45 Off-Road Rides in the Garden State

Mountain Biking in New Jersey

45 Off-Road Rides in the Garden State

Mountain Biking in New Jersey

By Christopher Mac Kinnon

REVISED AND EXPANDED EDITION

ISBN 0-9714616-3-5

FREEWHEELING PRESS
P.O. Box 540
Lahaska PA 18931

www.freewheelingpress.com
info@freewheelingpress.com

Special thanks

To my father, for instilling in me an appreciation for the simplicity of the natural world.

To Cathy, for believing in this project.

And to the many county, state, and federal park employees who took the time to answer questions and review the trail routes.

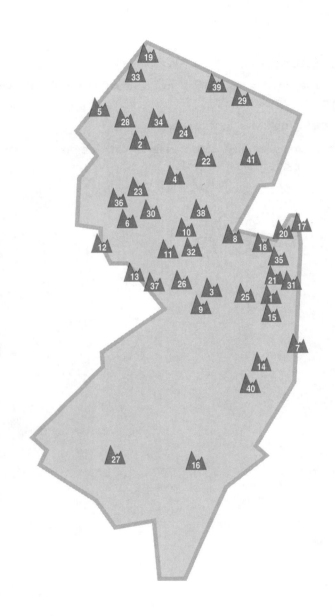

Contents

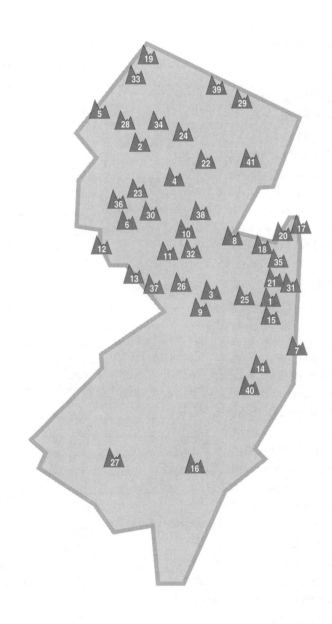

Christopher Mac Kinnon

About the author

Christopher Mac Kinnon, a resident of Wall Township, N.J., enjoys both road and mountain biking and has completed several century rides.

His passion for finding new places to ride has taken him all over the Garden State, and his enthusiasm for sharing his discoveries led to this book.

He put his experience as a professional illustrator and graphic artist to good use in creating the maps that detail each route.

Keep it clean: A special feature of this book

One thing for sure about off-road bicycling: Dirt happens!

You can put your clothes through the washer and hose down your bike after a messy ride, but there's not much you can do to clean a book that's covered in mud and grit. This is definitely a case where prevention is the best cure.

Mountain Biking in New Jersey has been designed so you can remove the individual maps, if you wish, and take them with you on your ride. All the information you need to find the trailhead and follow the route is printed back-to-back on a single sheet for each ride.

The pages have been designed to fit into a standard clear map protector available from retailers specializing in outdoor gear or from some office-supply stores.

For information about obtaining digital files of these maps, e-mail us at **info@freewheelingpress.com** or write to:

Freewheeling Press
P.O. Box 540
Lahaska PA 18931

Introduction

New Jersey's sometimes under-appreciated natural beauty is nowhere as evident as on its off-road trails.

The state's landscapes are many and diverse. In central New Jersey, the coastal region gradually gives way to rolling hills in the interior. Northern coastal destinations offer glimpses of New York City, while locales in the northwestern section are characterized by mountainous terrain.

The Garden State's network of parks, recreation areas, forests, and public open spaces provides many diverse opportunities for the mountain-bike enthusiast.

From nearly flat rail trails to strenuous rocky hill climbs, the rides included in this book range in difficulty from easy to expert.

The casual rider will enjoy both the Paulinskill Rail Trail and the Delaware and Raritan Canal. Both of these historic trails, once used as transportation corridors, now serve as multi-use recreational trails for bikers, hikers, and equestrians.

Trails through Allaire State Park and Huber Woods County Park, characterized by uneven terrain, singletrack, rolling hills, and occasional trail obstacles, are well suited for the intermediate rider.

Round Valley Reservoir and Mahlon Dickerson Reservation are representative of routes for advanced riders. Steep, rocky climbs and descents, frequent trail obstacles, and water crossings are typical along these routes. Suspension is highly recommended.

The routes described represent a cross section of the off-road terrain in New Jersey. A concerted effort was made to evaluate the degree of difficulty for each respective route.

Factors such as trail length, current trail conditions, terrain, etc., were considered in the evaluation process. Before deciding on a route, take a moment also to consider your own level of fitness—this, too, is relevant to ride difficulty.

And then ...

Enjoy!

About the maps

Trail ratings

Easy

Terrain is generally flat to rolling. Routes follow wide doubletrack trails or dirt or paved trails. Occasional singletrack is possible. Trail surface ranges from cinders and packed dirt to pavement. Some areas of loose gravel and sand are possible.

Moderate

Terrain is generally rolling to hilly. Climbs and descents may be on singletrack. Trail surfaces include the above, plus small obstacles (log jumps, larger rocks, exposed roots). Expect a generally uneven trail surface.

Difficult

Terrain is generally hilly to steep and trails are primarily singletrack. Strenuous climbs and descents are likely. In addition to the small obstacles mentioned above, larger trail obstacles should be expected. Stream crossings and very rocky areas are likely. Occasional dismounts and portages may be necessary.

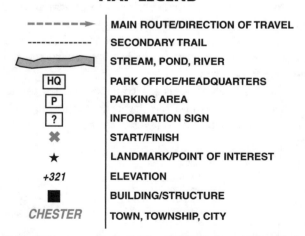

MAP LEGEND

- - - - - - →	MAIN ROUTE/DIRECTION OF TRAVEL
- - - - - - - -	SECONDARY TRAIL
	STREAM, POND, RIVER
HQ	PARK OFFICE/HEADQUARTERS
P	PARKING AREA
?	INFORMATION SIGN
✖	START/FINISH
★	LANDMARK/POINT OF INTEREST
+321	ELEVATION
■	BUILDING/STRUCTURE
CHESTER	TOWN, TOWNSHIP, CITY

Individual maps may also contain additional signs and symbols

14

Navigation

Realizing that many cyclists either do not have cyclo-computers or find their reliability questionable, I decided to include an approximate round-trip mileage for each ride instead of providing detailed point-to-point mileage readouts. I wanted those who use these maps to feel free to explore both the designated route and nearby points of interest without worrying about exact mileage figures. The maps include directional arrows as well as natural and man-made landmarks as navigational aids. In addition, each map includes a text box describing the route and the surrounding area.

I asked several fellow riders to follow the described routes, and I have incorporated their suggestions in the final version of the maps. Their consensus was that each map is descriptive of the respective route as well as informative.

The routes indicated on these maps depict trails that were open to mountain bikes at the time they were ridden. Personal riding habits as well as possible detours and trail conditions may affect trail mileage and ratings. Meeting the needs of the many and sometimes conflicting groups of trail users may result in policy changes regarding mountain-bike usage at each area.

Please abide by current posted information. When in doubt ... ask!

–Christopher Mac Kinnon

Trail openings and conditions are subject to change due to weather, rerouting, reclassification, or lack of maintenance. Please keep in mind that trails are multi-use; always yield to hikers and equestrians! The routes shown on these maps are not necessarily the only way through the respective areas. Please respect both private-property and trail-closure signs where posted.

Rules of the trail

Please ride cautiously! No matter how carefully a bicycling route is planned, it is impossible to eliminate all potential hazards or to foresee changes in trail conditions. Bicycle riding always involves a degree of risk.

International Mountain Bicycling Association

Rules of the trail

1. Ride on open trails only
2. Leave no trace
3. Control your bicycle
4. Always yield to non-bikers
5. Never spook animals
6. Plan ahead

and remember ...

... wear a helmet

... use courtesy and common sense

... trail riding is a privilege, not a right

... be supportive of trail-education efforts

... ride in small groups

... read posted trail signs and updates

Trail hazards:
Ticks & poison ivy

Scratches and bumps may be the most common physical afflictions endured by off-road cyclists, but the farther you go from wide, paved paths, the more likely you are to encounter the health threats posed by ticks and poison ivy, both of which are common in the woods and fields of New Jersey.

The state is part of a broad area where Lyme Disease is a growing health concern. This disease, caused by bacteria, can lead to arthritis and neurological disorders, among other problems. It is transmitted by the tiny deer tick, which is the size of a poppy seed in its nymphal stage and reaches the size of a sesame seed when fully grown.

Ticks can crawl onto you when you brush against grasses, shrubs, or other vegetation, or if you sit directly on the ground or on stone walls.

The American Lyme Disease Foundation recommends taking precautions to minimize the risk of acquiring the disease.

Unfortunately, many of the recommended defenses are more easily adopted by hikers than mountain bikers. Wearing light-colored, tightly woven long pants won't appeal to many cyclists, but the foundation also advises that you
- Scan clothes and any exposed skin frequently for ticks while outdoors
- Stay on cleared, well-traveled trails
- Use insect repellant containing DEET (Diethyl-meta-toluamide) on skin or clothes if you intend to go off-trail or into overgrown areas
- Do a final, full-body tick-check at the end of the day

Your chances of becoming infected with Lyme Disease are greatly reduced if you remove a tick within the first 24 hours. Early signs of Lyme Disease include flu-like symptoms and a characteristic "bull's-eye" rash, which can occur three days to a month after the tick bite. Consult your health-care professional with any concerns you might have about Lyme Disease.

Poison ivy is a less serious health threat, but it can make you mighty uncomfortable. Some commercial products can be applied before exposure to minimize the risk of getting the rash, but the first line of defense is to simply avoid contacting the poison ivy plant. The old saying "leaves of three, let it be" is good basic advice. If you are exposed, wash yourself as soon as you can. Plain cold water will help if you are near a stream or lake. Bathing with soap and warm water is even better, but the more time passes after you are exposed, the less effective that will be.

Remember that you can get the rash not only by brushing against the plant itself, but also by touching things that have come in contact with it, including your clothes and your bike. Consider giving them a good wash, too, if you think you've been through poison ivy.

Poison ivy

Wildlife Management Areas

A patchwork of Wildlife Management Areas scattered across New Jersey provides protected habitats for fish and wildlife as well as diverse opportunities for outdoor activities including mountain biking.

The Assunpink, Black River, Capoolong, and Lockwood Gorge rides in this book all pass through WMAs, which are administered by the New Jersey Division of Fish and Wildlife. The division's mountain-bike policy is designed to protect these areas as well as to coordinate the activities of cyclists and hunters.

According to the rules, mountain bikes are allowed within WMAs on all roads that are open to motor vehicles on a year-round basis. Bikes may also be used on trails and secondary roads from March 1 through April 15, June 1 through September 15, and on all Sundays. (Assunpink is an exception, however; bikes are allowed there on trails and secondary roads only between June 1 and August 30, and Sunday riding is permitted during that period only.)

Mountain bikes are barred from riding on dams, cultivated fields, and lawns in any WMA. Establishing new trails is also prohibited.

Sign at Allaire State Park

Allaire State Park

The restored 1830s village at Allaire State Park is a first-rate example of historical restoration. This old iron-making village has an outstanding collection of buildings and artifacts from this era, with guides in period costumes. It is definitely worth a look before or after your ride, but it is strictly for pedestrians—no bikes allowed.

A good portion of the park lies south of both the village area and the Manasquan River. This is where bicyclists are allowed on the multi-use trails, which are also frequented by hikers and equestrians. To get here from the village, go east on Route 524 for about 2 miles. Turn right onto Hospital Road. About 1 mile ahead there is a large gravel parking area on the right. Signs here provide trail updates and precautionary information regarding hunting and a persistent seasonal tick problem.

The updated trail-information map, provided courtesy of ATUG (Allaire Trail User Group), reflects recent renovations and designations at Allaire. Before three color-coded loop trails were marked in the park, it was relatively easy to become disoriented here. The new orange trail is about 4.6 miles long, the blue trail is 3.1 miles, and the white trail is 2.3 miles. Each offers a sample of what the area is like as a whole, including singletrack and wide fire roads and areas of "sugar sand" as well as hard-packed surface.

The orange trail continues past the point indicated on the route map and in fact is the outermost loop of the three. Unfortunately, it has some sections that are virtually unridable due to heavy concentration of sugar sand.

As you ride, you will notice many trail markings not indicated on the accompanying map. They are unreliable and perhaps outdated. Until you get to know the area, it is probably best to stick to the described route.

Since the area does have a reputation for ticks, we recommend that warm-weather riders make an effort to stay on the wider trails if possible, avoid areas that are wet or have tall grass, and wear light-colored clothing to make it easier to spot any ticks that have found you. We prefer to ride here in colder weather for two reasons: to avoid ticks, and also because there is a better chance that at least some of the sugar sand found here will have become hard-packed. See page 17 for more information on ticks.

Directions: From I-195, take Exit 31-B and go east on Route 524. Continue past the main park entrance. About 1.5 miles further, turn right onto Hospital Road. Go past the Edgar Felix parking area on your left. Cross the Manasquan River. Park at a large fenced area on your right.

TRAIL RATING: moderate
DISTANCE: apx. 7.6 miles
SURFACE: dirt, sand, gravel, pavement

reforestation area

overlook; first left after passing reforestation area

HOWELL TWP.

.5 miles to river; keep right at intersection

OW markings begin

green shed

W markings begin

eroded area

OW markings end

sand/gravel pit

B markings begin

O markings begin

Squankum Rd.

to I-195 FARMINGDALE

NOTE: NOT ALL INTERSECTIONS ARE DEPICTED ON MAP

park road

Hospital Rd.
to Rte. 34/Garden State Parkway

TRAILS

O	orange
OB	orange/blue
OW	orange/white
B	blue
W	white
U	unmarked

1 first loop
2 second loop

WALL TWP.

ALLAIRE STATE PARK

© Christopher Mac Kinnon 2003

TRAIL INFO: (FIRST LOOP) Orange Trail starts next to info sign. Crosses park road, continues to gravel/sand pit, following well-marked trail. Reach area with OB markings; continue following route. Trail splits; follow O markers. Reach second section of route marked OB. Trail splits; follow B. Reach 3-way intersection; go left on U trail (fire road). At 4-way intersection, go right, following O markings. O trail becomes OW. Follow to park road, turn right on road.

(SECOND LOOP) Right onto B trail. Trail splits at fire road; go left. Reach area with OB markings. Bear right where trail splits. Reach 4-way intersection. B goes left, then right again at next 4-way intersection (at this point following same route as first loop). At fire road, make a right; follow B markings to start of W trail at 4-way intersection. Trail ends at park road. Turn left on road; follow back to parking area.

Allamuchy Mountain State Park

Although neighboring Waterloo Village is the prime tourist attraction in the area and definitely worth a visit, it's the natural area at Allamuchy Mountain State Park that is of interest to the mountain biker.

Allamuchy is geologically similar to neighboring High Point State Park and Stokes State Forest, but the network of trails at Allamuchy avoids both the steepness and rocky trail surface characteristic of these parks.

The relatively isolated Deer Park Pond, which is along the described route, offers a quiet respite. Both bass and pickerel are to be found in its tranquil waters. The nearby Musconetcong River offers some of the best trout fishing in the state. Seasonal deer hunting is also allowed in the Allamuchy Natural Area; check posted information regarding seasonal openings and regulations.

Allamuchy's system of marked trails includes a section of the recently designated Highlands Trail. Please respect official trail-usage signs and, if necessary, refer to posted park maps for alternate routes.

The 19th-century Waterloo Village restoration, located on the Morris Canal and known for its summertime music performances, includes a working mill complex as well as a collection of historic buildings. Both the village (973-347-0900) and the park headquarters at adjacent Stephens State Park are located on nearby Waterloo Road (Route 604). The northern portion of Allamuchy park, which consists for the most part of rough unmarked trails, can be reached from Route 80 by exiting onto Route 206 north. Take the jughandle for International Drive and make a right at the first intersection. Follow this road for approximately 0.5 miles to a T-intersection at Waterloo Road. The heavily eroded parking area is straight across the intersection. This is also the southern terminus of a lightly used portion of the Sussex Branch Trail.

On your left as your ride along the rail trail, you'll find numerous steep and rough trails leading into Allamuchy's northern section. (Trails to the right generally lead to Jefferson Lake or the area around it.) Please respect posted private property signs in this area.

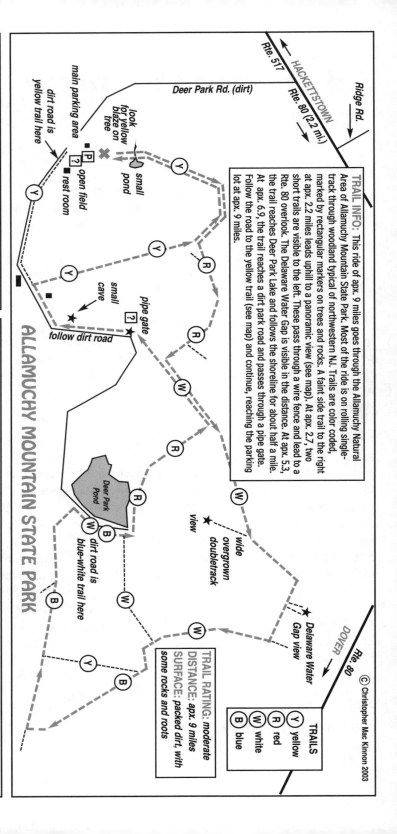

Allamuchy Mountain State Park
off Route 517
Hackettstown
Warren County
908-852-3790

Directions: From I-80, take Exit 19. Follow Route 517 south for about 2.2 miles. Turn left onto Deer Park Road (rough dirt road) and follow it to parking area.

TRAIL INFO: This ride of apx. 9 miles goes through the Allamuchy Natural Area of Allamuchy Mountain State Park. Most of the ride is on rolling single-track through woodland typical of northwestern NJ. Trails are color coded, marked by rectangular markers on trees and rocks. A faint side trail to the right at apx. 2.2 miles leads uphill to a panoramic view (see map). At apx. 2.7, two short trails are visible to the left. These pass through a wire fence and lead to a Rte. 80 overlook. The Delaware Water Gap is visible in the distance. At apx. 5.3, the trail reaches Deer Park Lake and follows the shoreline for about half a mile. At apx. 6.9, the trail reaches a dirt park road and passes through a pipe gate. Follow the road to the yellow trail (see map) and continue, reaching the parking lot at apx. 9 miles.

ALLAMUCHY MOUNTAIN STATE PARK

Rte. 80 (2.2 mi.)
HACKETTSTOWN
Rte. 517
Ridge Rd.

Deer Park Rd. (dirt)

main parking area
dirt road is yellow trail here

look for yellow blaze on tree

small pond

P
? open field
? rest room

small cave

pipe gate
follow dirt road

Deer Park Pond

dirt road is blue-white trail here

wide overgrown doubletrack
view

Delaware Water Gap view

DOVER
Rte. 80

TRAIL RATING: apx. 9 miles
DISTANCE: apx. 9 miles
SURFACE: packed dirt, with some rocks and roots

TRAILS
Y yellow
R red
W white
B blue

© Christopher Mac Kinnon 2003

Assunpink Wildlife Management Area

The Assunpink Wildlife Management area is located in extreme western Monmouth County, in the approximate geographic center of the state.

Despite its proximity to encroaching development, it is still a haven for wildlife native to the area, as well as a stopover for migrating birds. Assunpink's 5,700 acres offer many attractions to the human population as well. The name Assunpink is said to have originated from a Lenape Indian word that can be translated "rocky place that is watery." A network of artificial lakes resulting from the damming of Assunpink Creek provides excellent fishing opportunities. Chain pickerel and crappies are among the many species to be found here. Seasonal hunting and field trials are also popular at Assunpink. (See page 19 for more information on the WMA system, including the New Jersey Fish and Wildlife Division's official policies on riding in these areas.)

Although the terrain on some sections of this ride is similar to that found several miles south at Clayton County Park, the route was designed with the casual rider in mind. It uses the area's network of unpaved and paved roads. Both are open to vehicular traffic. County Route 524 is a light to moderately used country road, popular with area bike clubs.

A short section of the route follows one of the many wooded paths to be found in the area. It is indicated on the map east of the regional Wildlife Management Area office. If heavy rain or summer overgrowth makes the trail difficult to ride, you can bypass it by continuing past the gate until you reach the WMA office, then turning left onto the paved road also shown on the map.

Note: This area is also popular with equestrians and has many trails intended for horses. These equestrian trails can be easily identified by manmade obstacles, low fences, log piles, stone walls, and so forth. In the interest of both courtesy and safety, cyclists are encouraged to avoid the equestrian trails.

Assunpink Wildlife Management Area
Clarksburg-Robbinsville Rd.
Robbinsville
Monmouth County
609-259-2132

Directions: From I-95, take Exit 11 and follow signs to Xo's Corner via Imlaystown-Hightstown Road. At stop sign, cross Route 524. At next stop sign, cross Herbert-East Branch Roads. Continue to parking area.

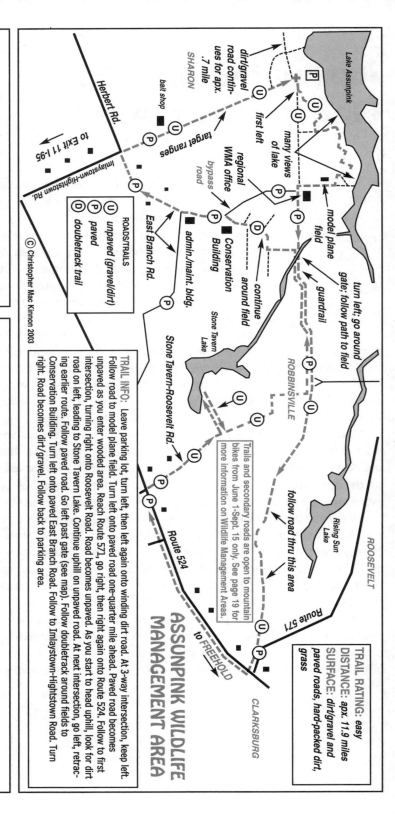

dirt/gravel road contin-ues for apx. .7 mile

SHARON

bait shop

first left

many views of lake

Herbert Rd.

to Exit 11 I-95

Imlaystown-Hightstown Rd.

target ranges

regional WMA office

bypass road

East Branch Rd.

ROADS/TRAILS
Ⓤ unpaved (gravel/dirt)
Ⓟ paved
Ⓓ doubletrack trail

Conservation Building

admin./maint. bldg.

continue around field

Lake Assunpink

model plane field

turn left; go around gate; follow path to field

guardrail

Stone Tavern Lake

Stone Tavern-Roosevelt Rd.

© Christopher Mac Kinnon 2003

ROBBINSVILLE

follow road thru this area

ROOSEVELT

Rising Sun Lake

Route 524

to FREEHOLD

Route 571

CLARKSBURG

ASSUNPINK WILDLIFE MANAGEMENT AREA

Trails and secondary roads are open to mountain bikes from June 1-Sept. 15 only. See page 19 for more information on Wildlife Management Areas.

TRAIL RATING: *easy*
DISTANCE: *apx. 11.9 miles*
SURFACE: *dirt/gravel and paved roads, hard-packed dirt, grass*

TRAIL INFO: Leave parking lot, turn left, then left again onto winding dirt road. At 3-way intersection, keep left. Follow road to model plane field. Turn left onto paved road one-quarter mile ahead. Paved road becomes unpaved as you enter wooded area. Reach Route 571, go right, then right again onto Route 524. Follow to first intersection, turning right onto Roosevelt Road. Road becomes unpaved. As you start to head uphill, look for dirt road on left, leading to Stone Tavern Lake. Continue uphill on unpaved road. At next intersection, go left, retracing earlier route. Follow paved road. Go left past gate (see map). Follow doubletrack around fields to Conservation Building. Turn left onto paved East Branch Road. Follow to Imlaystown-Hightstown Road. Turn right. Road becomes dirt/gravel. Follow back to parking area.

Black River Wildlife Management Area

State-owned fish and game lands constitute a sizable portion of the public land holdings in New Jersey. They are distinctly different in planning and purpose from state parks or state forests.

The state-issued guidebook to these areas that have been set aside for hunting and fishing describes little in the way of established trails or facilities. Navigation is at best difficult, and perhaps intentionally so.

The Black River Wildlife Management Area just north of Chester is more conducive to mountain biking than most. Here you will find two obvious paths that serve as the main arteries through the area. The first is the well-maintained rail trail that parallels the Black River. Uphill from it and running in a similar direction is a primitive utility road used to service power lines. Most of the described route makes use of these two trails.

Centrally located at Black River is a shotgun range, and you can expect to hear resounding echoes from the facility as you pedal along the route. A section of the utility road excluded from the described ride passes directly below the area; this route has been laid out to avoid it.

Although the ride is rated as intermediate overall, the rail trail is suitable for all riders. Traffic is minimal on the rail trail at Black River, even on weekends, and practically non-existent on both the utility road and connecting trails.

The nearby village of Chester, at the intersection of Routes 24 and 206, is bustling with activity on weekends. Quaint shops, boutiques, and eateries line its attractive main street.

(See page 19 for more information on the WMA system, including the New Jersey Fish and Wildlife Division's official policies on riding in these areas.)

Black River Wildlife Management Area

off Route 206
Chester
Morris County
908-879-6252

Directions: From Route 206 in Chester, turn east onto Route 24. About 0.3 miles ahead, turn left onto Hillside Avenue. Bear right at the intersection of Hillside and Pleasant Hill Road. Follow Pleasant Hill Road to the bottom of the hill. Look for a small parking area to the right, just before the road crosses the Lamington River. Additional parking is available on the other side of the bridge.

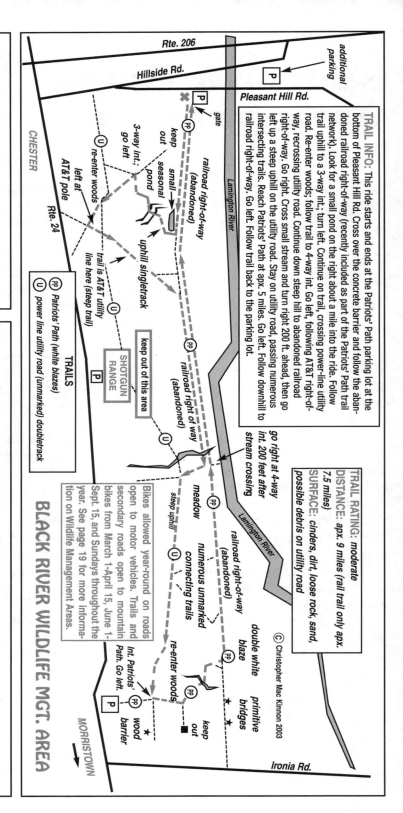

TRAIL INFO: This ride starts and ends at the Patriots' Path parking lot at the bottom of Pleasant Hill Rd. Cross over the concrete barrier and follow the abandoned railroad right-of-way (recently included as part of the Patriots' Path trail network). Look for a small pond on the right about a mile into the ride. Follow trail uphill to a 3-way int.; turn left. Continue on trail, crossing power-line utility road. Re-enter woods; follow trail to 4-way int. Go left, following AT&T right-of-way, recrossing utility road. Continue down steep hill to abandoned railroad right-of-way. Go right. Cross small stream and turn right 200 ft. ahead, then go left up a steep uphill on the utility road. Stay on utility road, passing numerous intersecting trails. Reach Patriots' Path at apx. 5 miles. Go left. Follow downhill to railroad right-of-way. Go left. Follow trail back to the parking lot.

TRAIL RATING: *moderate*
DISTANCE: *apx. 9 miles (rail trail only apx. 7.5 miles)*
SURFACE: *cinders, dirt, loose rock, sand, possible debris on utility road*

© Christopher Mac Kinnon 2003

CHESTER

Rte. 206

Hillside Rd.

Pleasant Hill Rd.

additional parking

P

P

gate

keep small out seasonal pond

3-way int.; go left

re-enter woods

left at AT&T pole

Rte. 24

railroad right-of-way (abandoned)

uphill singletrack

trail is AT&T utility line here (steep trail)

Lamington River

keep out of this area

SHOTGUN RANGE

P

railroad right of way (abandoned)

TRAILS

PP Patriots' Path (white blazes)
U power line utility road (unmarked) doubletrack

go right at 4-way int. 200 feet after stream crossing

meadow

steep uphill

railroad right-of-way (abandoned)

Lamington River

Bikes allowed year-round on roads open to motor vehicles. Trails and secondary roads open to mountain bikes from March 1-April 15, June 1-Sept. 15, and Sundays throughout the year. See page 19 for more information on Wildlife Management Areas.

numerous unmarked connecting trails

re-enter woods

double white blaze

primitive bridges

Int. Patriots' Path. Go left.

wood barrier

keep out

MORRISTOWN

Ironia Rd.

BLACK RIVER WILDLIFE MGT. AREA

Blue Mountain Lake

When North Jersey mountain-bike destinations are discussed, the names of places like Wawayanda, Ringwood, and Round Valley usually come up—and deservedly so, because these areas actively promote and encourage mountain biking on their trails.

The Delaware Water Gap, on the other hand, conjures up images of river canoeing, campfires, and hiking—and, of course, the spectacular vista of the gap itself, where the Delaware River curves its way magnificently through a set of ridges in the Pocono Mountains. Until recently, bikes were permitted only on paved roads within the Delaware Water Gap National Recreation Area. In an effort to expand recreational opportunities, however, the National Park Service has opened up the Blue Mountain Lake area to bikes.

The trails here provide access to an area that is slowly returning to its natural state, and they are usually well traveled, especially on summer and foliage-season weekends. Since mountain biking is a recently designated activity at Blue Mountain Lake, be sure to check the information board located next to the parking lot for postings about further expansion to the existing routes or new restrictions.

Trails here can get a bit overgrown, so summertime riders might wish to bring insect repellent and consider wearing long pants. Also, the area is somewhat isolated, but there is a toll-free 24-hour number for reporting emergencies or conservation violations: 800-543-4295.

If you wish to expand your two-wheeled outing, stop by the Kittatinny Point Visitor Center, located on Route 80, for information about the many lightly traveled paved roads throughout the park. If you have time, you can also pay a visit to the nearby re-created late-19th-century rural community at Millbrook Village for a journey into the past. This period village, circa 1880, is located at the intersection of Old Mine Road, Blairstown-Millbrook Road (Route 602), and Flatbrookville-Millbrook Road (see trail map).

BLUE MOUNTAIN LAKE

STAY ON MAIN TRAIL
THROUGH POND AREA
all other trails closed to bikes

pond view ★

Hemlock Pond

T

TRAIL INFO: This trail provides access to both Blue Mtn. Lake and Hemlock Pond. The route starts next to the information sign at the parking lot. Follow the singletrack trail to the right. (SLOW RIDING AREA!) About 100 yards ahead, reach a distinct 4-way intersection (see inset). Continue straight on rough road. Pass Blue Mtn. Lake on left. Arrive at 3-way intersection; make right uphill. Turn left at second intersection to begin loop (see map). Follow route to Hemlock Pond. Make loop around lake, staying on marked trail. Follow indicated route back to parking area.

no marker; make loop around pond

swampy area

loop

T

this trail shown as black dotted line on park map

T 4

T 3

loop starts at 4th marker (left downhill)

T 2

T

T T T

T T

T T } 1

multi-directional marker

black dash line trails may be unmaintained and overgrown

follow trail markers to 3-way intersection

inset

4-way int.

trail maps

to lake

[?]

[?]

★

★

gate

P

Blue Mtn. Lake Rd.

WALPACK TWP

Blue Mtn. Lake

T

T

T

T

see inset [?]

P

TRAIL RATING: *moderate*
DISTANCE: *apx. 6.8 miles*
SURFACE: *dirt, loose gravel, some larger rocks*

general store ★

Blue Mtn. Lake sign

Blue Mtn. Lake Rd.

to FLATBROOKVILLE/Rte. 206

Flatbrookville-Millbrook Rd.

to BLAIRSTOWN (Rte.80)

MILLBROOK VILLAGE

Blairstown-Millbrook Rd. (Rte. 602)

to Delaware Water Gap(Rte.80)

Old Mine Rd.

© Christopher Mac Kinnon 2003

Notes:

Capoolong Creek Wildlife Management Area

Just over 2 feet deep and perhaps 20 feet wide in spots, Capoolong Creek meanders through central Hunterdon County before emptying into the South Branch of the Raritan River. An aerial view would show it as a pretty ribbon winding through several rural communities.

Running along the creek from Pittstown to Landsdowne is a long, narrow wildlife management zone marked with numerous posted signs. The Capoolong Creek Wildlife Management Area, one of 126 WMAs in New Jersey, serves as a buffer zone to development. (See page 19 for more information on the WMA system, including the New Jersey Fish and Wildlife Division's official policies on riding in these areas.)

Not as well known as neighboring Lockwood Gorge, another WMA, it nonetheless is also popular with fishermen—and a satisfying destination for the casual rider.

The wildlife management area encompasses what was once a branch of the Lehigh Valley Railroad, a fact that is evidenced by lingering railroad bridges, embedded ties, and even a train station, now in disrepair. The rail trail is a little over 3 miles long, relatively flat, and quite lovely as it winds along beside the creek. This is not a challenging ride by any means, but the scenery makes it worth the effort.

As a curiosity, the name Capoolong has several variant spellings and is sometimes seen as Cakepoulin on various maps and road signs.

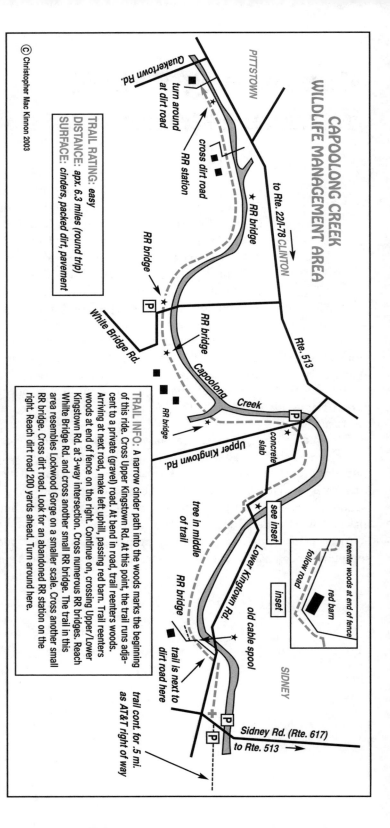

CAPOOLONG CREEK
WILDLIFE MANAGEMENT AREA

PITTSTOWN

Quakertown Rd.

to Rte. 22/I-78 CLINTON

turn around at dirt road

cross dirt road

RR station

RR bridge

RR bridge

Rte. 513

White Bridge Rd.

RR bridge

Capoolong Creek

RR bridge

RR bridge

Upper Kingtown Rd.

concrete slab

see inset

tree in middle of trail

Lower Kingtown Rd.

RR bridge

old cable spool

trail is next to dirt road here

SIDNEY

trail cont. for .5 mi. as AT&T right of way

Sidney Rd. (Rte. 617)

to Rte. 513 →

inset

reenter woods at end of fence

follow road

red barn

© Christopher Mac Kinnon 2003

TRAIL RATING: *easy*
DISTANCE: apx. 6.3 miles (round trip)
SURFACE: *cinders, packed dirt, pavement*

TRAIL INFO: A narrow cinder path into the woods marks the beginning of this ride. Cross Upper Kingstown Rd. At this point, the trail runs adjacent to a private (gravel) road. At bend in road, trail reenters woods. Arriving at next road, make left uphill, passing red barn. Trail reenters woods at end of fence on the right. Continue on, crossing Upper/Lower Kingstown Rd. at 3-way intersection. Cross numerous RR bridges. Reach White Bridge Rd. and cross another small RR bridge. The trail in this area resembles Lockwood Gorge on a smaller scale. Cross another small RR bridge. Look for an abandoned RR station on the right. Reach dirt road 200 yards ahead. Turn around here.

Directions: From I-78, get off at Exit 15. Take Route 513 south about a half mile to Sidney Road. Bear left on Sidney Road and follow it to the Capoolong Creek. Park on either side of the road on the south side of the creek.

Capoolong Creek Wildlife Mgt. Area
Sidney to Pittstown
Hunterdon County
609-984-0547

Cattus Island County Park

Bicycling at Cattus Island County Park is just one of many activities available at this bayside recreation facility. Slide shows, boat trips, and guided nature walks are among the programs open to the public at Cattus Island, which is actually a peninsula jutting out into Barnegat Bay.

The area has been preserved thanks to the foresight of a number of environmentally concerned individuals including the Cooper family, after whom the Cooper Environmental Center is named. Cattus Island provides a view back in time showing how much of the bay area once looked, and it exists today as both a reminder of the past and a shining example of ecosystem preservation.

The park's 500 acres of salt marshes and wetlands contain 6 miles of well-marked trails, but unfortunately the trail system at Cattus has been designated for foot travel only, and these are off limits to bicycling. Cyclists are allowed on the dirt road that runs through the park, which is short but definitely worth including in your visit. The road is closed to vehicular traffic, flat, and relatively smooth, making it ideal for even the most novice rider.

No visit to Cattus would be complete without a walk through the nature center. Here you will find hands-on displays ranging from area topographic maps to antique bay paraphernalia to artwork depicting wildlife native to the park. A well-versed staff of county naturalists and volunteers is available to answer questions.

During the warm-weather months, be sure to bring insect repellant—you'll find a large population of flies and mosquitoes among Cattus Island's many inhabitants!

Cattus Island County Park
off Fischer Boulevard
Toms River
Ocean County
732-270-6960

Directions: From the Garden State Parkway, take Exit 82 onto Route 37 east. Follow Route 37 for about 3 miles to the intersection of Fischer Boulevard. Take Fischer north, crossing back over Route 37. Follow Fischer for about 2.5 miles. At the traffic light, turn right onto Cattus Island Boulevard, then left into the park.

Barnegat Bay

TRAIL RATING: *easy*
DISTANCE: *apx. 2 miles (round trip)*
SURFACE: *dirt road, pavement*

road ends; turn around

osprey pole ★

Silver Bay

bay/wetland view

bay/wetland view

osprey pole ★

dirt road

★ mansion site

★ osprey pole

CATTUS ISLAND COUNTY PARK

bay/wetland view

bay/wetland view

pavement ends; follow dirt road

HQ
Environmental Center
← paved path
?
P

park entrance road

Cattus Isl. Blvd.

TRAIL INFO: Although only about 2 miles in length, this ride through the coastal woodlands and wetlands of Cattus Island County Park has much to offer. Be sure to stop at the Cooper Environmental Center, which has exhibits illustrating the importance of safeguarding this and other valuable wetlands. Look for a brown wooden sign near the paved walkway leading from the parking area to the nature center. To the left of it is a short connecting path leading to the paved road, where you begin and end this ride.

Fischer Blvd.   to Rte. 37/Garden State Pkwy.

to Hooper Ave
BRICK TWP.

BIKES ARE PERMITTED ONLY ON THE DIRT ROAD AT CATTUS ISLAND. ALL TRAILS ARE CLOSED TO BIKES.

DOVER TWP.

© Christopher Mac Kinnon 2003

Cheesequake State Park

Cheesequake State Park offers a rare off-road opportunity in an area of the state that is congested and, for the most part, paved over. Although most of the park's trails are off limits to mountain biking, Cheesequake's location and terrain make it a worthwhile destination. Trail usage is light to moderate, which is surprising considering the relatively high population and scarcity of other mountain-biking trails in the immediate area.

In contrast to the gently rolling grassy areas adjacent to the trailhead parking lot, the multi-use trail where mountain biking is permitted is surprisingly technical in spots, with numerous short but steep ascents and descents.

Trail marking is usually a hit-or-miss proposition. The white directional disks secured to trees are well intended but somewhat unreliable. Booth Field Road is the main artery through this section of the park. If you do get disoriented, use it to find your way back to the trailhead. It's a good idea to get a copy of the official park map because it shows Museum Road and many paved roads through the park that are worth exploring.

Park activities are geared toward family recreation and outdoor education. Refer to the multi-colored trail map at the trailhead for the location of the interpretive center off Museum Road. Hooks Creek Lake offers seasonal bathing, with nearby picnic facilities. Reserved campsites are available on a seasonal basis.

A word of caution: The Garden State Parkway commuter lot, which is visible at the end of Booth Field Road, is patrolled by the state police. Don't use it to get to the park, and don't park there.

TRAIL INFO: Park at the first lot on your left after entering the park, and follow park roads to the beginning of the multi-use trail on Booth Field Rd. Although the trail is marked "multi-use trail, State of New Jersey," the markings are inconsistent and at some points confusing. Use Booth Field Rd. to navigate. Museum Rd. (paved/dirt), which begins at the parking lot, leads to both the park interpretive center and Steamboat Landing, a leisurely round trip of about 3.5 miles. The large upright map next to the parking lot and the official park map both show this route. In spite of its short length, the multi-use trail has much to offer in the way of narrow singletrack, log jumps, and short but steep climbs and descents. Directional signs to Cheesequake State Park can be found on the Garden State Pkwy. (Exit 120), Rtes. 34 and 35, and the Laurence Harbor Pkwy. (Matawan Rd.).

Directions: From the Garden State Parkway, take Exit 120. Turn south on Matawan Road (also called Laurence Harbor Parkway). Follow it to the traffic light and turn right onto Morristown Road. Bear right at the next light onto Gordon Road and follow it to the park entrance. Go past the toll booth and park in the first lot on the left.

Cliffwood Rd.

to Rte. 34

OLD BRIDGE

Gordon Rd.

Laurence Harbor Pkwy.

Exit 120

left at wood post

follow road here

re-enter woods

ravines ★

TRAIL RATING: *moderate*
DISTANCE: *apx. 3.5 miles*
SURFACE: *dirt, gravel road, roots, pavement*

Gordon Rd.

Booth Field
outhouses

pavement ends here; trail continues on gravel/dirt road

Garden State Pkwy.

Booth Field Rd.

steep uphill ★

follow paved road back to parking lot

★ large log

follow road here

toll booth (seasonal)

park entrance road

Museum Rd. *(to Steamboat Landing)*

go past gate

multi-use trail starts here

Booth Field Rd

? HQ ★

open field

to multi use trail

(dirt)

gate ★

P ★
trail sign

(paved) (dirt)

© Christopher Mac Kinnon 2003

ALL TRAILS OTHER THAN THE MULTI-USE TRAIL ARE CLOSED TO BIKES

trail to Hooks Creek Lake apx. 0.5 mile

CHEESEQUAKE STATE PARK

Clayton County Park

Clayton County Park is proof that good things do indeed sometimes come in small packages. Although relatively small in size at 390 acres, the park is well suited for intermediate riders as well as less-experienced riders looking to upgrade their skills.

Clayton Woods is one of the least developed sites in the Monmouth County Park System. Located in Upper Freehold Township, the westernmost, least-populated part of Monmouth County, it is also one of the most isolated.

Clayton is about halfway between Mercer County Park to the west and Allaire State Park to the east, and it features the best aspects of both areas. Here you can find the hilly terrain of Allaire minus the sand, as well as the hard-packed singletrack characteristic of Mercer.

You can extend your day's outing by exploring the lightly trafficked country roads in the area. Old barns and horse farms dot the landscape in this part of Monmouth County, and despite recent development in the area, it still retains a rural atmosphere.

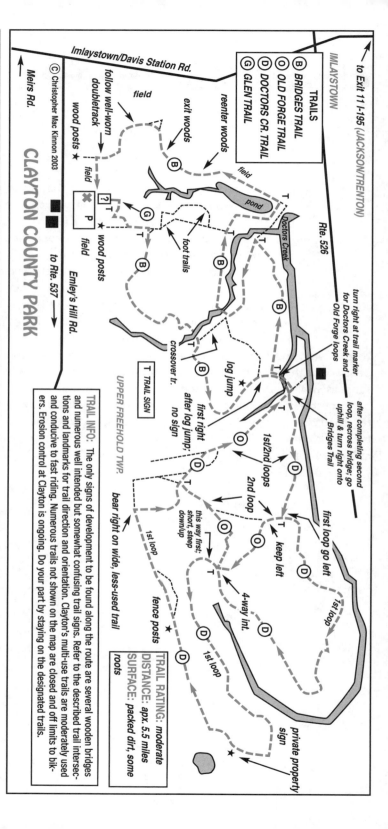

CLAYTON COUNTY PARK

TRAILS

- Ⓑ BRIDGES TRAIL
- Ⓞ OLD FORGE TRAIL
- Ⓓ DOCTORS CR. TRAIL
- Ⓖ GLEN TRAIL

© Christopher Mac Kinnon 2003

Ⓣ TRAIL SIGN

UPPER FREEHOLD TWP.

TRAIL INFO: The only signs of development to be found along the route are several wooden bridges and numerous well intended but somewhat confusing trail signs. Refer to the described trail direction and orientation. Clayton's multi-use trails are moderately used and conducive to fast riding. Numerous trails not shown on the map are closed and off limits to bikers. Erosion control at Clayton is ongoing. Do your part by staying on the designated trails.

TRAIL RATING: moderate
DISTANCE: apx. 5.5 miles
SURFACE: packed dirt, some roots

Clayton County Park
Emley's Hill Road
Upper Freehold
Monmouth County
732-842-4000

Directions: From I-195, take Exit 11 and follow Imlaystown-Hightstown Road (Route 43) south to stop sign. Turn left onto Route 526 and immediately turn right onto Davis Station Road. Follow Davis Station Road through Imlaystown, bearing right at the Happy Apple Inn. Continue past the lake on the left. About 0.6 miles ahead turn left onto Emley's Hill Road. Parking for Clayton County Park is about 0.3 miles further ahead on the left.

Delaware and Raritan Canal

Words such as placid, tranquil, and relaxing only begin to describe the atmosphere that is pervasive along the Delaware and Raritan Canal.

The canal is living testimony to the thousands of Irish immigrants who built it by hand between 1830 and 1834. When completed, it linked Bordentown in the south with New Brunswick to the north and served as an artery for transportation before the development of a widespread railroad system. Far removed now from its historic past, the Delaware and Raritan Canal today meets the needs of the surrounding area as a multi-use recreational facility suitable for canoeing, hiking, biking, fishing, and horseback riding. It also serves as a source of drinking water.

Although the mule-drawn barges are long gone, the towpath they trod still exists, and for much of its length it has been preserved as a New Jersey state park. It stands as a monument to historical foresight and preservation. This 35-mile greenway offers the longest continuous off-road opportunity for the New Jersey cyclist. With minimal interruptions you can ride from Alexander Road in Princeton to just south of the Route 18 bridge across the Raritan River in New Brunswick.

On its way, the canal passes through a number of small towns and villages, including Princeton, Griggstown, and Kingston. You can also find evidence of a once-vibrant trade route along the towpath. Historic buildings are located along the canal in Kingston, Griggstown, and Blackwells Mills, and there are several locks that were used to facilitate barge movement along the route. Look for the 22-mile marker north of Route 518 (see map for location). This was the halfway point of the original canal as it ran from Trenton to New Brunswick.

Canoe rentals are available in Griggstown and Princeton. Griggstown is also home to the canal museum, located just to the left of the towpath as you head north (see map).

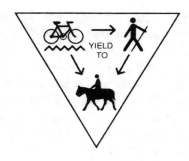

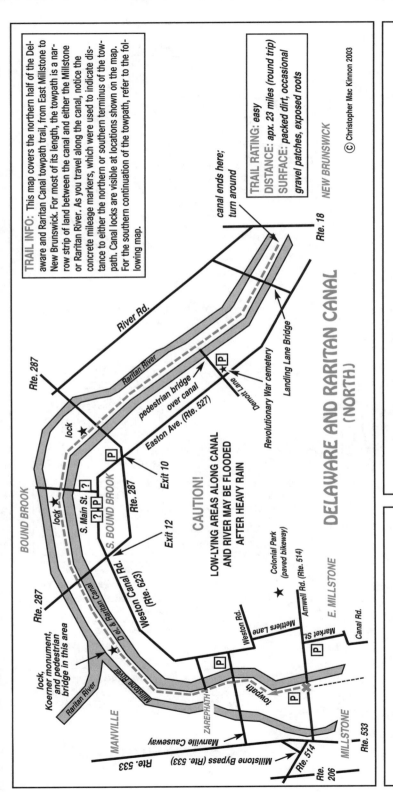

TRAIL INFO: This map covers the northern half of the Delaware and Raritan Canal towpath trail, from East Millstone to New Brunswick. For most of its length, the towpath is a narrow strip of land between the canal and either the Millstone or Raritan River. As you travel along the canal, notice the concrete mileage markers, which were used to indicate distance to either the northern or southern terminus of the towpath. Canal locks are visible at locations shown on the map. For the southern continuation of the towpath, refer to the following map.

TRAIL RATING: easy
DISTANCE: apx. 23 miles (round trip)
SURFACE: packed dirt, occasional gravel patches, exposed roots

© Christopher Mac Kinnon 2003

canal ends here; turn around

Rte. 18

NEW BRUNSWICK

River Rd.

Rte. 287

Raritan River

lock ★

pedestrian bridge over canal

Easton Ave. (Rte. 527)

P

Demott Lane

Revolutionary War cemetery

Landing Lane Bridge

BOUND BROOK

lock ★

S. Main St.

?

P

?

Rte. 287

P

Exit 10

S. BOUND BROOK

Exit 12

CAUTION!
LOW-LYING AREAS ALONG CANAL AND RIVER MAY BE FLOODED AFTER HEAVY RAIN

Weston Canal Rd. (Rte. 623)

Del. & Raritan Canal

Rte. 287

lock, Koerner monument, and pedestrian bridge in this area ★

Raritan River

Millstone River

MANVILLE

Millstone Bypass (Rte. 533)

Rte. 533

ZAREPHATH

Manville Causeway

P

Weston Rd.

Mettlers Lane

Colonial Park (paved bikeway) ★

Amwell Rd. (Rte. 514)

E. MILLSTONE

Market St.

Canal Rd.

P

towpath

P ✕

MILLSTONE

Rte. 514

Rte. 206

Rte. 533

DELAWARE AND RARITAN CANAL
(NORTH)

Directions: From Route 287, take Exit 12 to Weston Canal Road (Route 623) going south. Follow Weston Canal Road past Zarephath. Approximately 1.1 miles farther, turn left onto Weston Road before crossing the canal (there's an old white house on the corner). Follow Weston Road to Mettlers Lane. Turn right onto Mettlers. Turn right onto Mettlers Lane. Turn right onto Amwell Road (Route 514). Parking is on the right immediately after you cross the canal.

Delaware and Raritan Canal
East Millstone to New Brunswick
Somerset and Middlesex Counties
732-873-3050

Delaware and Raritan Canal
Princeton to East Millstone
Mercer and Somerset Counties
732-873-3050

Directions: From Route I, exit onto Alexander Road going west (toward Princeton). Follow for about 1 mile. Parking is available at Turning Basin Park on the left next to the canal.

TRAIL INFO: This flat out-and-back ride of approximately 29 miles along the canal towpath begins at Alexander Rd. off Rte. 1 near Princeton and reaches its northern terminus at Rte. 514 in East Millstone. (See the previous map for trail continuation.) Soon after the start of the ride, Carnegie Lake, used by Princeton University crew teams for rowing competition, is visible to the left. At Kingston, the towpath goes through a tunnel under Rte. 27. This is a good vantage point from which to observe the northerly flow of the Millstone River. The Flemer Trail, 100 yds. to the right off Rte. 27, is available as an optional route north to the Rte. 518 trail crossing (see map). Stop at the park office in Griggstown for more information.

Rte. 514

E. MILLSTONE

BLACKWELLS MILLS

B. Mills causeway

Delaware and Raritan Canal

Canal Rd.

park office
Six Mile
Run trail
(see separate map)

canal museum

GRIGGSTOWN

Rte. 533

22-mile marker

Griggstown causeway

Millstone River

Rte. 206

ROCKY HILL

Canal Rd.

Rte. 518

bridge tender's home
(partial reconstruction)

Flemer Trail

KINGSTON

trail goes under
Rte. 27 (tunnel)

Rte. 27

Rte. 27

Mapleton Rd.

Rte. 1

PRINCETON

Carnegie Lake

pedestrian bridge to towpath

aqueduct

Harrison St.

Washington Rd.
(Rte. 571)

Alexander Rd.

see inset

inset

turning basin

towpath

Alexander Rd.

Turning
Basin
Park

Canal

trail continues;
becomes singletrack

TRAIL RATING: *easy*
DISTANCE: *apx. 29 miles (round trip)*
SURFACE: *packed dirt, occasional gravel and roots*

© Christopher Mac Kinnon 2003

CAUTION!

LOW-LYING AREAS ALONG CANAL AND RIVER MAY BE FLOODED AFTER HEAVY RAIN

DELAWARE AND RARITAN CANAL
(SOUTH)

Notes:

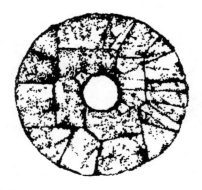

Old millstone along the Delaware and Raritan Feeder Canal

Delaware and Raritan Feeder Canal

Whether it qualifies as a true canal in the textbook sense of the word is subject to debate, but why bother? If it looks and feels like a canal, then relax and enjoy the ride.

The Delaware and Raritan Feeder Canal was originally constructed to provide water to the main canal, which is described in the previous chapter. But experiencing the feeder canal's diverse scenery, quaint crossroads, and agreeable trail surface is much more enjoyable than quibbling over the technical aspects of its construction. The feeder canal runs through the heart of an area that is enormously popular with tourists, and you'll find a series of interesting towns and worthwhile detours along the way.

Until a few years ago, the multi-use path beside the feeder canal was divided into two distinct sections. One ran from just north of Trenton to Lambertville, the other from just north of Lambertville to Frenchtown. Happily, however, the two sections have been joined, so it is now possible to ride the entire path straight through. For most cyclists interested in this type of ride, however, a jaunt covering part of the trail will suffice for a day's outing.

For variety, the Delaware Canal on the Pennsylvania side of the Delaware River also has a bikeable towpath. Bridges at Washington Crossing, Lambertville, Stockton, Bull's Island, and Frenchtown make it possible to cross the river and use the other towpath as an alternate return route.

The **Delaware and Raritan Feeder Canal (North)** map shows the route starting at Prallsville Mills, north of Stockton on Route 29. You might want to look through the restored mill and surrounding buildings and grounds during your visit. No longer operating as a working mill, this 19th-century building is often host to art shows, concerts, and private parties.

The atmosphere along this stretch of the canal is markedly different from the southern section. The feeling of being in the woods is strong here. Development is minimal along this portion of Route 29, and traffic is considerably lighter than around Lambertville and Washington Crossing. The wide shoulder along the road provides another safe alternate route for your return trip.

Include a short side trip to Bull's Island if time allows. The northern tip of the island marks the beginning point of the feeder canal. Follow the paved road past the park headquarters (left turn from the towpath if you're riding north) to the narrow pedestrian bridge that crosses the river. On the Pennsylvania side is the quaint village of Lumberville. North of Bull's Island, canal views are replaced by glimpses of the river to the left and ever-increasing rock outcroppings accompanied by soaring hawks to the right.

Frenchtown is an attractive riverside community where you can grab a bite to eat, relax, and enjoy the sights along the river before starting back.

The route detailed in the **Delaware and Raritan Feeder Canal (South)** map begins at New Jersey's Washington Crossing State Park, located at the intersection of Route 546 and River Road near the bridge across the Delaware River. The towns of Washington Crossing (there are two by that name, one in New Jersey and the other in Pennsylvania) are easily accessible from the trailhead parking area. If you take the bridge across the river to Washington Crossing, Pa., you'll find numerous historic buildings housing Revolutionary War memorabilia immediately to your right. Included are replicas of the boats used by George Washington during his fateful river crossing on Christmas night in 1776.

You can reach the main part of New Jersey's Washington Crossing State Park by walking your bike across the pedestrian overpass located adjacent to the trailhead. If time allows, include at least a visit to the park visitor center and Continental Lane. Another detour worth considering is the scenic riverside village of Titusville, shown on the map as an alternate return route.

In Lambertville, you can stop for refreshments or to visit some of the town's many antique shops, or venture across the river to New Hope. Art galleries, antiquing, fine dining, and everything but the ordinary only begins to describe a side trip to New Hope.

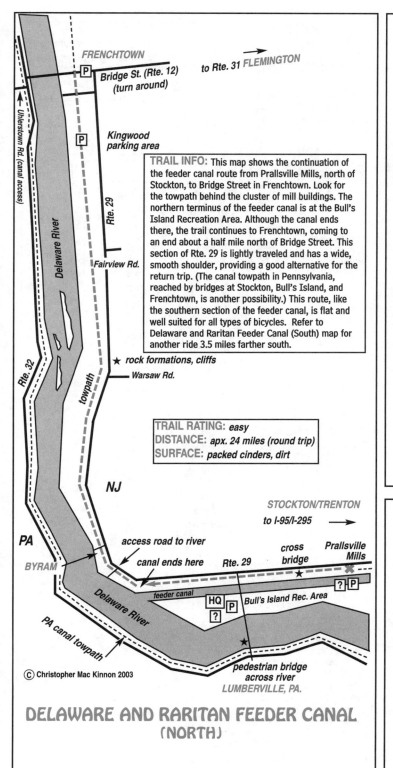

FRENCHTOWN

to Rte. 31 FLEMINGTON →

P Bridge St. (Rte. 12)
(turn around)

Uhlerstown Rd. (canal access) ←

Kingwood
parking area

P

Rte. 29

Delaware River

Fairview Rd.

TRAIL INFO: This map shows the continuation of the feeder canal route from Prallsville Mills, north of Stockton, to Bridge Street in Frenchtown. Look for the towpath behind the cluster of mill buildings. The northern terminus of the feeder canal is at the Bull's Island Recreation Area. Although the canal ends there, the trail continues to Frenchtown, coming to an end about a half mile north of Bridge Street. This section of Rte. 29 is lightly traveled and has a wide, smooth shoulder, providing a good alternative for the return trip. (The canal towpath in Pennsylvania, reached by bridges at Stockton, Bull's Island, and Frenchtown, is another possibility.) This route, like the southern section of the feeder canal, is flat and well suited for all types of bicycles. Refer to Delaware and Raritan Feeder Canal (South) map for another ride 3.5 miles farther south.

Rte. 32

towpath

★ rock formations, cliffs
— Warsaw Rd.

TRAIL RATING: *easy*
DISTANCE: *apx. 24 miles (round trip)*
SURFACE: *packed cinders, dirt*

NJ

STOCKTON/TRENTON

to I-95/I-295 →

PA

access road to river

cross bridge | Prallsville Mills

BYRAM

canal ends here | Rte. 29

? P

Delaware River

feeder canal

HQ P
?

Bull's Island Rec. Area

PA canal towpath

★

pedestrian bridge
across river
LUMBERVILLE, PA.

© Christopher Mac Kinnon 2003

DELAWARE AND RARITAN FEEDER CANAL
(NORTH)

Directions: From I-95 north of Trenton, exit onto Route 29 north (last exit in NJ). Follow Route 29 to Lambertville. At the traffic light in Lambertville, turn left onto Bridge Street. Turn right at the next light onto North Main Street to continue north on Route 29. Follow Route 29 through Stockton. About 0.5 miles ahead, look for the Prallsville Mills parking area on the left.

Delaware and Raritan Feeder Canal
Stockton to Frenchtown
Hunterdon County
609-397-2949

Delaware and Raritan Feeder Canal
Washington Crossing to Lambertville
Mercer and Hunterdon Counties
609-397-2949

Directions: From I-95 north of Trenton, exit onto Route 29 onto Route 29 north (last exit in New Jersey). Follow Route 29 north for about 2.5 miles to the intersection with Route 546. Turn left onto Route 546, then right onto River Road after you cross the canal. The parking lot will be immediately on your right.

NEW HOPE
Rte. 29
Bridge St.
Rte. 179
LAMBERTVILLE

TRAIL RATING: *easy*
DISTANCE: *apx. 14 miles (round trip)*
SURFACE: *cinders, dirt, pavement*

see Lambertville inset

© Christopher Mac Kinnon 2003

wing dam

Rte. 518
(to Rte. 206)
PRINCETON →

river access

★

Bowman's Hill Tower (Revolutionary War lookout)

Rte. 32

PA canal towpath

Delaware River

towpath

feeder canal

Rte. 29

inset
Lambertville area

Bridge St.

turn around here

PA canal towpath

Delaware River

feeder canal

P

★ lock

DELAWARE AND RARITAN FEEDER CANAL (SOUTH)

TRENTON

TITUSVILLE

Washington Crossing State Park (see separate map)

Church St.

Rte. 29

Delaware River high-water mark (on tree) 6/20/55 →

★

WASHINGTON CROSSING, NJ

Rte. 546

River Rd.

NJ

P

PA

towpath

TRAIL INFO: This ride of about 14 miles follows the canal towpath from Washington Crossing to Lambertville. It begins and ends at the parking area where Rte. 546 intersects River Rd. in Washington Crossing. (On the return trip, you can opt for an alternate route through Titusville via River Road; see map. The canal towpath in Pennsylvania, reached by bridges at Washington Crossing and Lambertville, is another possibility.) Directly across the river from Lambertville is New Hope, Pa., well known for its antique shops and art galleries. Refer to Delaware and Raritan Feeder Canal (North) map for another ride 3.5 miles farther north.

WASHINGTON CROSSING, PA

Notes:

Cranberry plant

Double Trouble State Park

Located southwest of Toms River on the edge of the New Jersey Pine Barrens, Double Trouble State Park is one of the highlights along the New Jersey Coastal Heritage Trail. Developed primarily for touring by car, the "trail" will link historic, cultural, and natural sites along a 300-mile route from Perth Amboy south to Cape May and from Cape May northwest to the Delaware Memorial Bridge.

Double Trouble got its start as a lumbering center in the 1860s, and at its peak as many as 2,500 people were employed there. Eventually, as the swamps were depleted of timber, they were turned into cranberry bogs. The cranberry industry became a vital part of the South Jersey economy toward the end of the 19th century, and at one time, New Jersey held the distinction of being the nation's leading producer of cranberries. (Today it ranks third behind Massachusetts and Wisconsin.)

The historic village at Double Trouble includes a restored sawmill and cranberry packing and sorting house, with several active cranberry bogs nearby. Other activities available at the park include a self-guided nature walk and canoeing on Cedar Creek. This ride goes through just a small portion of the 5,000-acre park on a wide, hard-packed dirt-and-gravel route that is suitable for all bikes with wide tires.

Trail brochures and information about the New Jersey Coastal Heritage Trail can by obtained by writing the New Jersey Division of Travel and Tourism at PO Box 820, Trenton NJ 08625-0820, or by calling 609-292-2470. The official Web site for the trail is at **http://www.nps.gov/neje/home.htm**.

DOUBLE TROUBLE STATE PARK

★ cedar forest

sawmill

see inset of village area

★ bridge

"Forest Mgt." sign; turn around here

TRAIL RATING: easy
DISTANCE: apx. 3.5 miles
SURFACE: packed dirt, gravel, some patches of sand

pedestrian trail

Cedar Creek

sorting-packing houses

bog

bog

bog

Double Trouble Rd.

reservoir

LACEY TWP.

reservoir

bridge

straight at int.

left at 5-way intersection

follow wide doubletrack

bog

bog

Pinewald - Keswick Rd.

BERKELEY TWP.

bridge

Garden State Pkwy.

© Christopher Mac Kinnon 2003

inset of village area
SLOW RIDING AREA

sawmill

maintenance bldg.

sorting-packing house

bog

gates

HQ

P

Pinewald - Keswick Rd.

Double Trouble Rd.

TOMS RIVER/Exit 80, GSP

TRAIL INFO: Leave the dirt parking lot. Pass through a gate and follow the wide dirt path through the village area. To the right is a building housing the park office and restrooms; literature pertaining to the park is available here. In the distance the sawmill is visible. Pristine Cedar Creek bisects the park and marks the boundary between Berkeley and Lacey Townships. The absence of any present-day development along the route serves to heighten the experience of a "forgotten" New Jersey, and you can let your mind wander back to a simpler time at Double Trouble.

DOUBLE TROUBLE IS AN ECOLOGICALLY SENSITIVE AREA. MANY PROTECTED AND ENDANGERED PLANTS ARE FOUND HERE. PLEASE STAY ON THE DESIGNATED TRAILS.

Double Trouble State Park
Pinewald-Keswick Rd.
Lacey and Berkeley Townships
Ocean County
732-341-6662

Directions: From the north, take the Garden State Parkway to Exit 80, turn left from the exit ramp, and take Double Trouble Road 3.5 miles to the stop sign. The park entrance will be straight ahead. From the south, take the parkway to Exit 74 and go east 0.8 miles on Lacey Road. Turn left onto Manchester Avenue, go half a mile, and make another left onto Western Boulevard. At the stop sign, turn left onto Route 618. Go west under the parkway bridge and left one half mile after the parkway into the park.

Edgar Felix Bikeway

The Edgar Felix Bikeway runs from Hospital Road in Wall Township to the seaside community of Manasquan in eastern Monmouth County. The route follows an abandoned railroad right-of-way, now paved. The smooth surface allows for use by all types of bicycles.

This is a moderately to heavily trafficked multi-use trail, and you can expect to encounter just about anything with two or more wheels along the way. It's a good idea to ride slowly. In many places, the path runs right next to private property, and local residents in the area seem to regard it as an extension of their own backyards.

The ride begins at the Hospital Road parking lot. Refer to the Allaire State Park map for additional trails in this area. If parking is a problem at the Hospital Road lot, you can opt to park at either the Allaire lot, about three-quarters of a mile down Hospital Road, or at the municipal parking area next to the gazebo by the general store in Allenwood.

Orchard Park, near the end of the route, contains tennis courts and a basketball court, as well as swings and a play area for children. Once you reach Manasquan, you can get to the beach area by turning right onto Main Street and following it downtown, crossing Route 71, and continuing to the beach.

Another approach to this ride is to park at the municipal lot on North Main Street in Manasquan and follow the route in reverse. Mountain bikers from the Manasquan-Brielle area use the Edgar Felix Bikeway as a connecting route to and from nearby Allaire State Park.

Plans are underway to extend the bikeway past the Spring Meadow Golf Course at Allaire State Park. Eventually, the bikeway is expected to go all the way to Trenton.

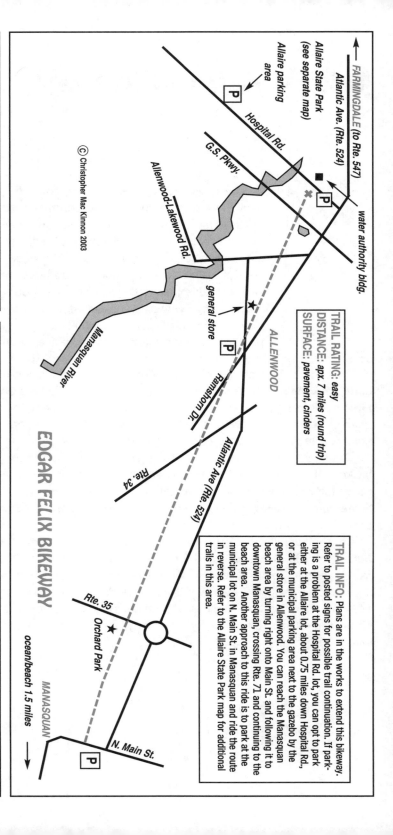

EDGAR FELIX BIKEWAY

Edgar Felix Bikeway
Wall Township to Manasquan
Monmouth County
732-449-8444

FARMINGDALE (to Rte. 547)

Atlantic Ave. (Rte. 524)

water authority bldg.

Allaire State Park
(see separate map)

Allaire parking
area

Hospital Rd.

G.S. Pkwy.

Allenwood-Lakewood Rd.

© Christopher Mac Kinnon 2003

Manasquan River

general store

ALLENWOOD

Ramshorn Dr.

Rte. 34

Atlantic Ave (Rte. 524)

Rte. 35

Orchard Park

MANASQUAN

ocean/beach 1.5 miles

N. Main St.

TRAIL RATING: *easy*
DISTANCE: *apx. 7 miles (round trip)*
SURFACE: *pavement, cinders*

TRAIL INFO: Plans are in the works to extend this bikeway. Refer to posted signs for possible trail continuation. If parking is a problem at the Hospital Rd. lot, you can opt to park either at the Allaire lot, about 0.75 miles down Hospital Rd, or at the municipal parking area next to the gazebo by the general store in Allenwood. You can reach the Manasquan beach area by turning right onto Main St. and following it to downtown Manasquan, crossing Rte. 71 and continuing to the beach area. Another approach to this ride is to park at the municipal lot on N. Main St. in Manasquan and ride the route in reverse. Refer to the Allaire State Park map for additional trails in this area.

Directions: From I-195, take Exit 31 and go east on Route 524 (Allaire Road-Atlantic Avenue). Continue past the main entrance to Allaire State Park. About 1.5 miles farther, turn right onto Hospital Road. You'll find the Edgar Felix parking area on your left.

Estell Manor County Park

Atlantic County usually brings to mind images of its most famous destination, Atlantic City, the gambling capital of the East. A visit there is likely to be a win-lose proposition at best.

Nearby Estell Manor County Park, on the other hand, is a sure winner. The nature center and historic points of interest have been drawing visitors for years. Hiking and boating are also popular activities. Now mountain biking can be added to this list.

The Duck Farm Trail, located in the north end of the park, is the end result of thoughtful planning and hard work by members of the Atlantic County Trail Volunteers organization (ACTV; see page 126 for more information about this organization). In 2002, ACTV received final approval to build a singletrack mountain bike route. Thanks to this new trail, a loop route totaling approximately 6 miles, Estell Manor is shaping up as the prime mountain-biking destination in South Jersey.

The trail is located along the coastal lowlands and elevation change is negligible but at the same time incidental, due to the creative layout of the route. A serpentine hard-packed path through a forest of pine, oak, and holly awaits riders of all abilities.

This is a trail built by dedicated mountain bikers for mountain bikers. Horses are prohibited on this trail and should be reported to the park office.

The nature center/park office located about a mile south on Route 50 can provide updated route maps as well as information regarding the park.

Estell Manor County Park
Route 50
Estell Manor City
Atlantic County
609-645-5960

Directions: From the south, take the Garden State Parkway to Exit 36. Go west on Route 40 about 11 miles to Route 50. Turn left and follow Route 50 south approximately 3 miles to the parking area on the left. From the north, get off at Exit 37, follow signs to Route 40, and proceed as above.

to MAYS LANDING →
Garden State Parkway

Rte. 50

ESTELL MANOR

old railroad bed ★

North End Tr.

end singletrack

T

North End Tr.

T trail marker

trail access

trail access

begin singletrack
DUCK FARM LOOP

T

TRAIL RATING: *easy*
DISTANCE: *apx. 5.4 miles*
SURFACE: *dirt, gravel, grass*

North End Tr.

T

info sign → ★

P

┼

inset

grass field

T

Artesian Well Road (dirt/gravel)

see inset for cont.

go around gate

parking area/trailhead

T

© Christopher Mac Kinnon 2003

sign/gate

★

main park entrance apx. 1 mile

TRAIL INFO: From the parking lot, follow Artesian Well Rd. back toward Rte. 50. After passing a grassy field on the right, look for a sign on the right indicating the North End Trail. Go around the gate, following wide doubletrack to the beginning of the Duck Farm singletrack loop, which is unmarked but obvious on the left about 50 yards past a North End Trail marker. Follow a twisty, hard-packed route with occasional log obstacles and dips along the way. The route eventually returns to the North End Trail, north of your initial entry point. Turn left, following abandoned railroad right-of-way. Here you will experience the unusual sensation of riding over railroad ties. Continue North End Loop. Follow described route back to parking area.

NOTE: A recent trail extension goes beyond the ride shown on this map. Check the park office for the latest map. All trails at the park except the Boardwalk Trail are open to bikes.

ESTELL MANOR COUNTY PARK

Hartshorne Woods County Park

Located near what is arguably the highest point on the eastern seaboard (Mount Mitchell, elevation 266 feet), Hartshorne Woods and the adjacent Twin Lights loom as sentinels overlooking the Atlantic Ocean. It's true, of course, that folks from eastern Maine might laugh at the idea of Mount Mitchell beating out Maine's 1,530-foot Cadillac Mountain for the title. But the New Jersey peak, located off Route 36 about 1.5 miles east of Hartshorne, rises right along the shoreline, offering wonderful views that reach as far as New York City.

Hartshorne can also boast or weep about its unofficial title as the facility most heavily used by bicyclists in the Monmouth County Park System.

What nearby Huber Woods County Park has on a small scale, Hartshorne has in abundance. Its reputation as a first-class mountain-bike destination is well deserved. A network of well-marked trails takes you through a heavily forested landscape via challenging singletrack. Expect long stretches of hard-packed fast trail, with just enough technical terrain to challenge your bike-handling skills. (Trails in Hartshorne Woods Park are multi-use, so you'll want to stay alert and slow down when approaching blind turns along the trail.)

Mountain-biking opportunities here have been enhanced by the addition of the Rocky Point Trail, a challenging route that explores the hills and valleys of the historic Rocky Point area. If time and energy permit, enjoy a detour that begins where you exit the Rocky Point Trail. A paved multi-use path passes numerous remnants of World War II gun batteries. There's a spectacular view of the Atlantic Ocean from atop the overlook at Battery Lewis. Refer to the posted map as well as trail brochures at the trailhead for further information.

A seasonal view of the Navesink River can be had from the Claypit Creek Overlook. After a steady climb of about a mile, look for a trail marker to the right indicating this overlook. A short trail leads to a vantage point where you can take a breather as well as view the sights along the river.

This ride starts at the Buttermilk Valley Trailhead on Navesink Avenue.

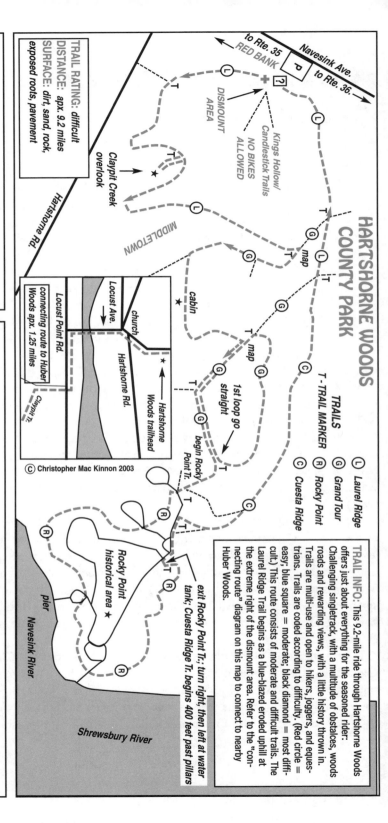

HARTSHORNE WOODS COUNTY PARK

Hartshorne Woods County Park
Navesink Avenue
Middletown
Monmouth County
732-842-4000

TRAIL RATING: difficult
DISTANCE: apx. 9.2 miles
SURFACE: dirt, sand, rock, exposed roots, pavement

TRAILS

T - TRAIL MARKER

(L) Laurel Ridge
(G) Grand Tour
(R) Rocky Point
(C) Cuesta Ridge

TRAIL INFO: This 9.2-mile ride through Hartshorne Woods offers just about everything for the seasoned rider: Challenging singletrack, with a multitude of obstacles, woods roads and rewarding views, with a little history thrown in. Trails are multi-use and open to hikers, joggers, and equestrians. Trails are coded according to difficulty. (Red circle = easy; blue square = moderate; black diamond = most difficult.) This route consists of moderate and difficult trails. The Laurel Ridge Trail begins as a blue-blazed eroded uphill at the extreme right of the dismount area. Refer to the "connecting route" diagram on this map to connect to nearby Huber Woods.

exit Rocky Point Tr.; turn right, then left at water tank; Cuesta Ridge Tr. begins 400 feet past pillars

Directions: From Route 35 north of Red Bank, turn east onto Navesink River Road. Follow road for about 2.7 miles, passing a golf course. Continue past Brown's Dock Road. Merge with Route 8A, passing Oceanic Bridge on your right. Turn right onto Locust Avenue and cross Claypit Creek. At a large stone church, bear right onto Navesink Avenue. The parking area for Hartshorne Woods is about 0.5 mile ahead on the right.

Navesink Ave.
to Rte. 35
RED BANK
to Rte. 36.
P
?

DISMOUNT AREA
NO BIKES ALLOWED
Kings Hollow/ Candlestick Trails

Claypit Creek overlook

Hartshorne Rd.

MIDDLETOWN

map

1st loop go straight

begin Rocky Point Tr.

Locust Woods connecting route to Huber Woods apx. 1.25 miles

Locust Ave.
Locust Point Rd.
church
Hartshorne Rd.
Hartshorne Woods trailhead
cabin
Claypit Tr.

© Christopher Mac Kinnon 2003

Rocky Point historical area

pier

Navesink River

Shrewsbury River

Notes:

Henry Hudson Trail

The Henry Hudson Trail is a prime example of the successful reclamation of a resource that had been allowed to fall into a state of disrepair.

The trail was once part of the Jersey Central Railroad, which closed its operations in the area in the mid-1960s. It was seriously neglected before it was finally taken over by the Monmouth County Parks System, which joined residents from the surrounding communities in bringing the abandoned transportation link back to prominence, this time without the once-mighty Iron Horse. Today, you are likely to encounter walkers, joggers, and roller skaters as well as fellow bike riders along the route, which is approximately 10.5 miles long.

The trail surface is paved, and bridges crossing several tidal creeks along the route have been rebuilt, providing views of the surrounding tidal marshes as well as distant glimpses of the lower Manhattan skyline. The trail serves the bayshore towns it runs through (including Keyport, Union Beach, Hazlet, and Keansburg) both as a recreational facility and as a pathway connecting neighborhoods and communities. Flat terrain and the smooth surface make this a good area for young or inexperienced riders.

The trail does continue on past the turn-around point designated on this route map (McMahon Park/Atlantic Avenue), but it comes increasingly closer to the noise and congestion of Route 36 and provides a less pleasant ride. A planned extension of the western end of the trail is expected to bring it through Matawan to Freehold in the next few years, adding another 12 miles to its overall length.

A word of caution: Although the Henry Hudson Trail is open only to non-motorized traffic, it does cross many roads along the way. Cyclists should be aware of traffic at these intersections.

HENRY HUDSON TRAIL

Henry Hudson Trail
Aberdeen to Atlantic Highlands
Monmouth County
732-842-4000

Directions: From the Garden State Parkway, take Exit 117. Turn left onto Clark Street. The trail access/parking area is just off the parkway at the intersection of Clark, Lloyd Road, and Gerard Avenue. Park at Fireman's Field across from the trailhead.

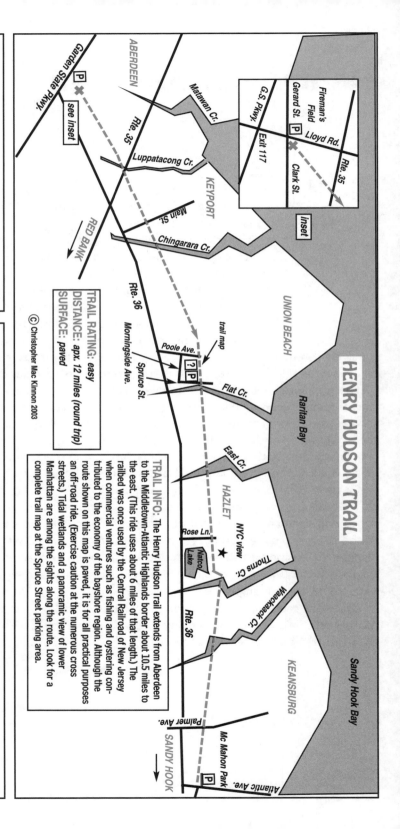

TRAIL RATING: *easy*
DISTANCE: *apx. 12 miles (round trip)*
SURFACE: *paved*

© Christopher Mac Kinnon 2003

TRAIL INFO: The Henry Hudson Trail extends from Aberdeen to the Middletown-Atlantic Highlands border about 10.5 miles to the east. (This ride uses about 6 miles of that length.) The railbed was once used by the Central Railroad of New Jersey when commercial ventures such as fishing and oystering contributed to the economy of the bayshore region. Although the route shown on this map is paved, it is for all practical purposes an off-road ride. (Exercise caution at the numerous cross streets.) Tidal wetlands and a panoramic view of lower Manhattan are among the sights along the route. Look for a complete trail map at the Spruce Street parking area.

ABERDEEN

KEYPORT

UNION BEACH

HAZLET

KEANSBURG

SANDY HOOK

Raritan Bay

Sandy Hook Bay

Garden State Pkwy.

RED BANK

Rte. 35

Matawan Cr.

Luppatacong Cr.

Main St.

Chingarara Cr.

Rte. 36

Morningside Ave.

Spruce St.

Poole Ave.

Flat Cr.

East Cr.

Rose Ln.

Natco Lake

Thorns Cr.

NYC view

Waackaack Cr.

Rte. 36

Palmer Ave.

Atlantic Ave.

Mc Mahon Park

P see inset

trail map

? P

inset

Fireman's Field

G.S. Pkwy.

Gerard St. P

Exit 117

Lloyd Rd.

Clark St.

Rte. 35

High Point State Park

The 220-foot monument that crowns the highest point in New Jersey (1,803 feet above sea level) is included in this ride through High Point State Park, which offers excellent tri-state views. To the north lie the Catskill Mountains of New York; to the west, the Pocono Mountains of Pennsylvania. Much of the woodland visible to the south is part of Stokes State Forest, which can be reached via the Parker Trail (refer to the trail maps for High Point and Stokes for the connecting route).

High Point lends itself to exploration by the moderately fit as well as those looking for a strenuous outing. This ride combines sections of pavement and well-marked primitive woods roads; while not technically challenging, these roads demand a high level of physical exertion. The area is not especially well maintained, and downed trees and long rocky stretches characterize parts of these trails. For those who prefer a more leisurely ride, the park's excellent network of paved roads offers several miles of pleasurable riding opportunities.

Caution: The section of the Deckertown Turnpike (Route 650) between the Big Flatbrook and the intersection of the Appalachian Trail is quite steep. Stop by the park office for route suggestions.

Boating, fishing, and swimming are popular seasonal activities at High Point. Both the Lake Marcia and monument areas are likely to be crowded on warm-weather weekends. On the other hand, it is possible to ride long stretches of this route without encountering another rider, even when the park is relatively busy.

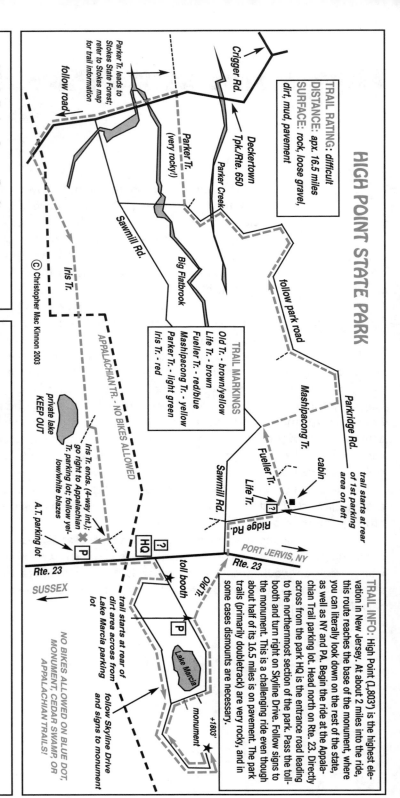

HIGH POINT STATE PARK

TRAIL RATING: *difficult*
DISTANCE: *apx. 16.5 miles*
SURFACE: *rock, loose gravel, dirt, mud, pavement*

Crigger Rd.

Deckertown Tpk./Rte. 650

Parker Creek

Parker Tr. (very rocky!)

Sawmill Rd.

Big Flatbrook

Parker Tr. leads to Stokes State Forest; refer to Stokes map for trail information

follow road

© Christopher Mac Kinnon 2003

Iris Tr.

follow park road

Parkridge Rd.

Mashipacong Tr.

trail starts at rear of 1st parking area on left

cabin

Fueller Tr.

Life Tr.

?

Ridge Rd.

Sawmill Rd.

PORT JERVIS, NY

Rte. 23

TRAIL MARKINGS
Old Tr. - brown/yellow
Life Tr. - brown
Fueller Tr. - red/blue
Mashipacong Tr. - yellow
Parker Tr. - light green
Iris Tr. - red

APPALACHIAN TR. - NO BIKES ALLOWED

private lake
KEEP OUT

Iris Tr. ends (4-way int.); go right to Appalachian Tr. parking lot; follow low/white blazes

A.T. parking lot

Iris Tr. parking lot; follow yellow blazes

✗

P

HQ

?

Rte. 23

SUSSEX

toll booth

Old Tr.

P

Lake Marcia

+1803'

monument

trail starts at rear of dirt area across from Lake Marcia parking lot

follow Skyline Drive and signs to monument

NO BIKES ALLOWED ON BLUE DOT, MONUMENT, CEDAR SWAMP, OR APPALACHIAN TRAILS!

TRAIL INFO: High Point (1,803') is the highest elevation in New Jersey. At about 2 miles into the ride, this route reaches the base of the monument, where you can literally look down on the rest of the ride, as well as NY and PA. Begin the ride at the Appalachian Trail parking lot. Head north on Rte. 23. Directly across from the park HQ is the entrance road leading to the northernmost section of the park. Pass the toll-booth and turn right on Skyline Drive. Follow signs to the monument. This is a challenging ride even though about half of its 16.5 miles is on pavement. The park trails (primarily doubletrack) are very rocky, and in some cases dismounts are necessary.

High Point State Park
Route 23
Sussex
Sussex County
973-875-4800

Directions: Take Route 23 north through Sussex and continue for about 7 miles. Park at the Appalachian Trail parking area located about 150 yards south of the High Point State Park office.

Huber Woods County Park

At about 250 acres, Huber Woods County Park is one of the smallest parcels of land included in this guide. In spite of its relatively small size, however, Huber is a worthwhile off-road destination for a number of reasons, the first being location. It is relatively close to both Hartshorne Woods County Park and the Henry Hudson Trail, and, in addition, it offers the ideal combination of terrain for expert riders to enjoy or for intermediate riders to upgrade their bike-handling skills.

Using the connecting Claypit Run Trail (one of the few soft-sand trails at Huber), many riders combine the trail systems at Huber and Hartshorne Woods. There are enough trails in the two parks to make for a full-day outing. (Refer to the Hartshorne Woods map for the connecting route between these two areas.)

Also, what Huber Woods lacks in size it more than makes up for in trail accessibility. The vast majority of the park's trails are open to bikes, the exception being the nature loop clearly marked at the point where you first enter the woods. Finally, Huber Woods offers a variety of trails, almost all singletrack, ranging from the relatively easy Fox Hollow to the moderately difficult Many Log Run, which probably is the trail most prized by bikers. To these advantages you can add highly visible trail markings, a hard-packed surface, and the allure of the woods itself.

Trails at Huber are primarily multi-use and are color coded according to difficulty. Any attempt to evaluate trail difficulty involves a degree of subjective opinion, but the three categories used here do seem to represent three distinct degrees of difficulty. Look for trail markers at most major intersections. Green circles mark the easiest trails, primarily used by pedestrian traffic, blue squares indicate medium difficulty, and black diamonds are used for the most difficult trails.

Huber Woods trails contain many stretches with blind curves. The park is moderately to heavily used, and cyclists can expect to encounter both equestrian and foot traffic on all the trails.

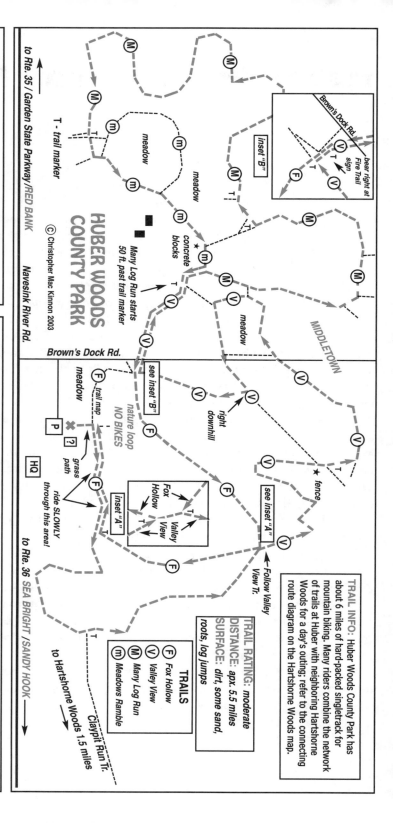

Huber Woods County Park
Brown's Dock Road
Locust
Monmouth County
732-842-4000

Directions: From Route 35 north of Red Bank, head east onto Navesink River Road and go about 2.7 miles. Pass a golf course. Turn left onto Brown's Dock Road (bumpy dirt road). Parking area is about 0.4 miles ahead on the right.

to Rte. 35 / Garden State Parkway/RED BANK

T - trail marker

© Christopher Mac Kinnon 2003

Navesink River Rd.

HUBER WOODS COUNTY PARK

Many Log Run starts 50 ft. past trail marker

meadow

concrete blocks

MIDDLETOWN

Brown's Dock Rd.

Inset "B"

bear right at Fire Trail sign

Brown's Dock Rd

see inset "B"

nature loop
NO BIKES

right downhill

meadow

trail map

grass path

ride SLOWLY through this area

Inset "A"

Fox Hollow
Valley View

see inset "A"

Follow Valley View Tr.

fence

to Rte. 36 SEA BRIGHT / SANDY HOOK

to Hartshorne Woods 1.5 miles

Claypit Run Tr.

TRAIL INFO: Huber Woods County Park has about 6 miles of hard-packed singletrack for mountain biking. Many riders combine the network of trails at Huber with neighboring Hartshorne Woods for a day's outing; refer to the connecting route diagram on the Hartshorne Woods map.

TRAIL RATING: moderate
DISTANCE: apx. 5.5 miles
SURFACE: dirt, some sand, roots, log jumps

TRAILS
Ⓕ Fox Hollow
Ⓥ Valley View
Ⓜ Many Log Run
ⓜ Meadows Ramble

Joe Palaia Township Park

A casual rider friend introduced me to Joe Palaia Township Park. Unable to persuade him to venture to either Allaire or Cheesequake, I agreed to meet him here. Several laps around the well-designed 3-mile circuit trail provided a nice change of pace from the serious workouts at other locations nearby.

The park has an interesting history. The property was first developed as a farm, and a well-preserved mastodon skeleton, since lost, was discovered there in the early 19th century. Later known as the Deal Test Site, it was used for communications purposes by AT&T, and three tall towers used to communicate with ships still stand. Later still, it was used by the Army in tracking satellites. It was purchased by Ocean Township in the early 1970s and was subsequently developed as a park.

Half of the park is open space and the other half is covered with vegetation including a swamp forest, wetlands, and an area of seashore vegetation. The area is popular with birders in May and September. There is an osprey nest on one of the towers, and ospreys have been seen hunting for fish nearby.

Joe Palaia Township Park
Deal Road
Ocean Township
Monmouth County
732-531-5000

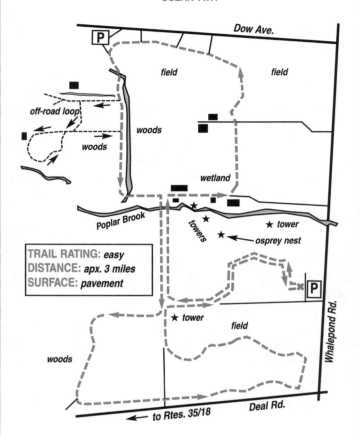

OCEAN TWP.

Dow Ave.

P

field

field

off-road loop

woods

woods

wetland

Poplar Brook

towers

★ tower

★ osprey nest

P

Whalepond Rd.

★ tower

field

woods

← to Rtes. 35/18

Deal Rd.

TRAIL RATING: *easy*
DISTANCE: *apx. 3 miles*
SURFACE: *pavement*

© Christopher Mac Kinnon 2003

TRAIL INFO: Joe Palaia's well-planned loop trail invites the casual rider to explore its network of wide paved trails. This is a multi-use area popular with neighborhood joggers, roller bladers, and bicyclists. Trails are flat and well maintained. Suitable for all bikes and riding levels. A short (apx. 0.3-mile) unmarked off-road loop using both double and singletrack trails is indicated on the route map. Begin and end your ride at the main parking area off Whalepond Rd.

JOE PALAIA TOWNSHIP PARK

Directions: From the south, take Route 18 north to Exit 11A (Deal Road). Follow Deal Road east, crossing Route 35 in 0.8 miles. The park is half a mile past Route 35 on the left. From the north, take Route 18 south to Exit 12A (West Park Avenue) and go east 0.3 miles to Poplar Road. Turn right onto Poplar and follow it 0.8 miles to Deal Road. Turn left onto Deal, cross Route 35, and continue to the park.

Notes:

Trail information sign at Lewis Morris County Park

Lewis Morris County Park

This ride at Lewis Morris County Park begins and ends at the Sunrise Lake parking lot, which serves as the focal point for a variety of park activities, including swimming, boating, and fishing, as well as mountain biking. Cyclists will find easy access here to the network of park trails including Patriots' Path (see separate maps).

Figuring out which trails are actually open to bicycles can be confusing, however. The official 1993 park map does not indicate the redesignation of several trails including the yellow "mountain-bike trail." To get the latest information on trails, cyclists should refer to updated posted information, which might include a revised map. Also, neighboring Morristown National Historic Park limits bike usage to paved roads. Look for posted signs along the Lewis Morris route around milepost 3.9 indicating the boundary line between the two parks. A portion of the Patriots' Path, which is included in the Lewis Morris route, is also closed to bikes once it crosses into Morristown National Historic Park.

Trail usage at Lewis Morris ranges from moderate to heavy, and conflicts may occur. While not as physically demanding as Mahlon Dickerson Reservation, Lewis Morris does have its share of trail obstacles and varied surfaces, loose gravel, exposed roots, and occasional wet spots. In conjunction with Patriots' Path, it can provide a full-day outing for the intermediate-level rider.

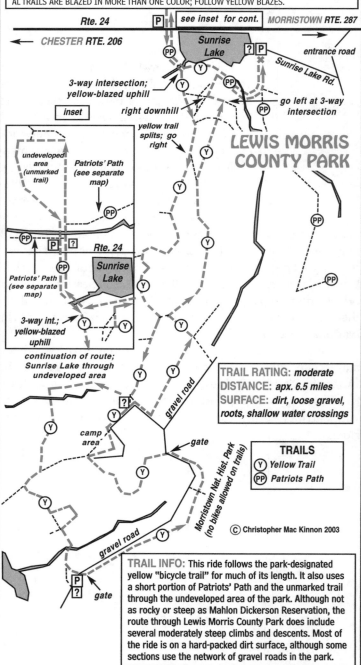

Lewis Morris County Park
Route 24
Morris Township
Morris County
973-326-7600

Directions: From I-287, take Exit 35 and follow Route 24 west through Morristown and around the green. The park entrance is on the left approximately 3.5 miles past Morristown.

SUNRISE LAKE AREA: This ride begins and ends at the Sunrise Lake parking area. Look for the "no outlet" sign at the far end of the lot, opposite Rte. 24. Follow paved trail through the picnic area (RIDE SLOWLY HERE). Pavement ends at the bottom of the hill; intersect white-blazed Patriots' Path. Go right; follow gravel/dirt path. Cross small stream. Yellow blazes start 50 ft. ahead. This is where you will eventually come out again on Patriots' Path. (Refer to the inset of the undeveloped area of the park for trail continuation.) After riding the undeveloped section, follow Patriots' Path back to 3-way intersection. Go right up yellow-blazed steep doubletrack SEVERAL TRAILS ARE BLAZED IN MORE THAN ONE COLOR; FOLLOW YELLOW BLAZES.

Rte. 24   P ↑↑   see inset for cont.   MORRISTOWN RTE. 287

← CHESTER RTE. 206

Sunrise Lake

entrance road

Sunrise Lake Rd.

3-way intersection; yellow-blazed uphill

go left at 3-way intersection

right downhill

inset

yellow trail splits; go right

LEWIS MORRIS COUNTY PARK

undeveloped area (unmarked trail)

Patriots' Path (see separate map)

Rte. 24

Sunrise Lake

Patriots' Path (see separate map)

3-way int.; yellow-blazed uphill

continuation of route; Sunrise Lake through undeveloped area

gravel road

camp area

gate

Morristown Nat. Hist. Park (no bikes allowed on trails)

gravel road

gate

TRAIL RATING: *moderate*
DISTANCE: *apx. 6.5 miles*
SURFACE: *dirt, loose gravel, roots, shallow water crossings*

TRAILS
Y *Yellow Trail*
PP *Patriots Path*

© Christopher Mac Kinnon 2003

TRAIL INFO: This ride follows the park-designated yellow "bicycle trail" for much of its length. It also uses a short portion of Patriots' Path and the unmarked trail through the undeveloped area of the park. Although not as rocky or steep as Mahlon Dickerson Reservation, the route through Lewis Morris County Park does include several moderately steep climbs and descents. Most of the ride is on a hard-packed dirt surface, although some sections use the network of gravel roads in the park.

Lockwood Gorge/ Columbia Trail

As the South Branch of the Raritan River winds its way through Hunterdon County, its demeanor changes, gradually at first, then abruptly south of the village of Califon. Rolling farmland and gently sloping banks give way to a rugged landscape as you enter the Ken Lockwood Gorge, aptly named after an environmental visionary who was instrumental in preserving the area.

For the next 2 miles, the landscape is characterized by jagged rock outcroppings and steep forested walls populated by evergreens. The once-placid Raritan changes its temperament as well as it rushes noisily over and around rocks and boulders of varying sizes and shapes. This section of the river is treasured as one of the state's prime fly-fishing areas.

(See page 19 for more information on the WMA system, including the New Jersey Fish and Wildlife Division's official policies on riding in these areas.)

This route takes you beside the river and through the gorge via Raritan River Road, as well as above the gorge via the Columbia Rail Trail. The combination of a tree-shaded trail and the opportunity to enjoy the cooling effects of the river make this an ideal destination for a leisurely ride on a hot summer day.

An old iron bridge and the railroad station that now serves as the Califon Museum add both atmosphere and history to the village of Califon. The Califon Museum (see map for location), built in 1875, houses a collection of railroad memorabilia and Americana and is open from 1 to 3 P.M. on the first and third Sundays of the month between May and December.

Parking is available in High Bridge at the Borough Commons municipal lot or along the trail itself off Mill Street (see map insert for locations).

The route initially begins as an unmaintained dirt road between Main Street and Mill Street and soon goes under a bridge. After passing several houses, the trail narrows and parallels the river, eventually crossing it.

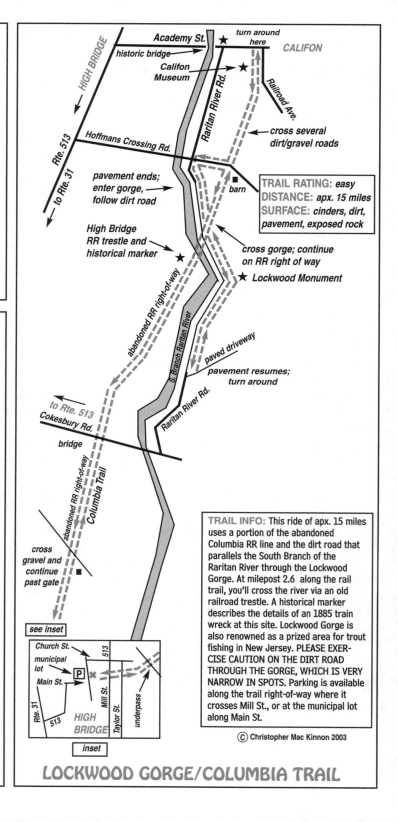

Lockwood Gorge/Columbia Trail
High Bridge to Califon
Hunterdon County
908-782-1158

Directions: From I-78, exit onto Route 31 north. About 2 miles north of I-78, turn right onto Route 513. Follow West Main Street (Route 513) under a railroad bridge and turn left to continue on Route 513. Turn right onto Church Street (still Route 513) and continue to the intersection with Mill Street. Park along the trail right-of-way on Mill Street or at the municipal lot on Main Street.

HIGH BRIDGE

Academy St.
turn around here
CALIFON
historic bridge
Califon Museum
Raritan River Rd.
Railroad Ave.
cross several dirt/gravel roads
Rte. 513
Hoffmans Crossing Rd.
to Rte. 31
pavement ends; enter gorge, follow dirt road
barn

TRAIL RATING: *easy*
DISTANCE: *apx. 15 miles*
SURFACE: *cinders, dirt, pavement, exposed rock*

High Bridge RR trestle and historical marker
cross gorge; continue on RR right of way
★ Lockwood Monument

abandoned RR right-of-way
S. Branch Raritan River
paved driveway
pavement resumes; turn around
Raritan River Rd.

to Rte. 513
Cokesbury Rd.
bridge
abandoned RR right-of-way
Columbia Trail

cross gravel and continue past gate

see inset

TRAIL INFO: This ride of apx. 15 miles uses a portion of the abandoned Columbia RR line and the dirt road that parallels the South Branch of the Raritan River through the Lockwood Gorge. At milepost 2.6 along the rail trail, you'll cross the river via an old railroad trestle. A historical marker describes the details of an 1885 train wreck at this site. Lockwood Gorge is also renowned as a prized area for trout fishing in New Jersey. PLEASE EXERCISE CAUTION ON THE DIRT ROAD THROUGH THE GORGE, WHICH IS VERY NARROW IN SPOTS. Parking is available along the trail right-of-way where it crosses Mill St., or at the municipal lot along Main St.

Church St.
municipal lot
P
Main St.
Rte. 31
513
513
Mill St.
Taylor St.
underpass
HIGH BRIDGE

inset

Ⓒ Christopher Mac Kinnon 2003

LOCKWOOD GORGE/COLUMBIA TRAIL

Mahlon Dickerson Reservation

With over 3,000 acres, the Mahlon Dickerson Reservation seems more like a state forest than a county-run facility. Deer, beaver, and black bear are among the animals that reside in this heavily wooded reservation.

Located in northwestern Morris County, it is generally regarded as the number-one mountain-bike destination within the Morris County Park System. In addition to the yellow trail, which is officially designated for bike use, the route described here uses several other trails, including the white-blazed Pine Swamp Trail, the green-blazed Boulder Trail, and the 2.5-mile Edison Branch Rail Trail, originally known as the Ogden Mine Railroad, built to serve iron mines in the area. Highlights of the ride include picturesque Saffin Pond and the highest elevation in Morris County (1,395 feet).

Mahlon Dickerson's system of marked trails includes a section of the recently designated Highlands Trail. Please respect official trail-usage signs and, if necessary, refer to posted park maps for alternate routes.

Trail usage is generally light to moderate here, for several reasons. First, most trails at Mahlon Dickerson can be classified as difficult, the exception being the Edison Branch Rail Trail. Also, the park is located in the less populated part of Morris County. (A small portion of the rail trail extends into neighboring Sussex County.) And finally, the size of the park means that there are more than enough trails to accommodate many riders.

In addition to the described route, many other loop rides are possible. Refer to park-posted maps at Saffin Pond and the information board shown on the map insert. Morris County trail maps are among the most reliable in accurately representing both trail configurations, updates, and the locations of structures and geographical features.

Note: Trail usage and designation are currently being debated by various groups of trail users. At the time of publication, the Morris County Parks Commission was trying to develop a solution acceptable to all parties. It is likely that this process will affect several parks in the Morris County system, including Mahlon Dickerson, Patriots' Path, and Lewis Morris. Before beginning your ride, check the information sign at the Saffin Pond parking lot for the latest developments.

Sparta Mtn. Rd.

right onto blue/white tr.

trail sign for white-blazed Pine Swamp Tr.

follow white and blue blazes here

4-way int.; turn right onto unmarked doubletrack

right onto Pine Swamp Tr. (white)

elev. sign

trail sign

1395 +
highest elevation in Morris Co.

white tr. goes left (long downhill)

intersect boulder tr. (green)

pass several singletrack trails

abandoned RR bed (trail)

Toomeys Pond

Weldon Rd.

Saffin Pond

intersect yellow tr.; go left

follow unmarked doubletrack

no bikes this section

Headley overlook

overlook

very steep downhill

tr. briefly follows rocky singletrack

resume doubletrack

TRAIL RATING: *difficult*
DISTANCE: *apx. 8.5 miles*
SURFACE: *dirt, cinders, exposed roots, large rocks, water crossings, pavement*

stone foundation

Crane Rd.

steep downhill

Weldon Rd.

abandoned RR bed (trail)

to Rte. 15 / I-80 DOVER

yellow blazes resume

yellow tr. goes left; follow unmarked doubletrack

TRAILS

(Y) *yellow Bike Trail*
(G) *green Boulder Trail*
(W) *white Pine Swamp Trail*
(H) *blue Highlands Trail (also marked with diamond symbol)*

wood posts; turn right; yellow markers resume

follow paved road

re-enter woods; follow yellow singletrack

MAHLON DICKERSON RESERVATION

© Christopher Mac Kinnon 2003

inset

ball field

picnic area

paved path

Weldon Rd.

see inset

TRAIL INFO: A bike with suspension is highly recommended for this ride! Expect to encounter lengthy sections of trail characterized by steep climbs and descents over bone-shaking rock. If you're familiar with the multi-use trail at Round Valley, you'll have a good idea of what to expect. Part of the ride follows the blue-blazed Highlands Trail, although the portion of it south of Weldon Road is closed to bikes (see map). A side trip on foot to the Headley Overlook provides a rewarding view of near wilderness, with Bowling Green Mtn. visible in the distance straight ahead and a portion of Lake Hopatcong visible in the distance to the right.

PLEASE RIDE SLOWLY THROUGH THE AREA SHOWN ON THE MAP INSET. THIS IS A HEAVILY USED DAY SECTION OF THE PARK.

Manasquan Reservoir

In addition to providing a supply of drinking water, Manasquan Reservoir serves as a wildlife habitat and recreation area for southern Monmouth County.

This ride follows the perimeter trail, which is approximately 5 miles long and mostly level with a few gradual inclines. The ride begins and ends at the main park entrance road. From the parking lot, backtrack towards the tollbooth. The trail crosses the entrance road at a diagonal 25 feet before the toll. Look for a small sign indicating the trail entrance, and bear right, following the trail.

A number of unmarked side trails intersect the obvious wide main cinder/dirt trail. If you travel in a clockwise direction as indicated by the directional arrows on the map, trails to the right of the main route head in the direction of the reservoir; trails to the left lead either to private property or to one of the surrounding perimeter roads.

The reservoir, which is adjacent to the Howell Park Golf Course, is a great place for a family outing, with a number of other activities besides bicycling available to round out the day.

Bird watching is a popular activity in the park, and the Chestnut Point parking area is a well known fishing spot. From this area, an eerie forest of dead trees rises from the waters of the reservoir. Non-motorized boats can be launched for a small fee, and rowboats and kayaks can be rented. Guided boat tours are also available. Check at the park office for details.

Caution: Weekend use at Manasquan Reservoir ranges from moderate to heavy. The perimeter trail is multi-use and traveled in both directions. Along the route there are numerous blind corners. Ride with care!

Manasquan Reservoir
Windeler Road
Howell Township
Monmouth County
732-842-4000

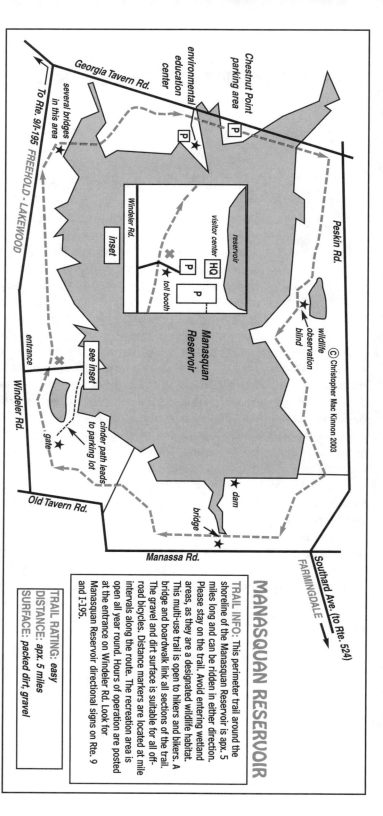

Chestnut Point parking area

environmental education center

Georgia Tavern Rd.

To Rte. 9/I-195

FREEHOLD - LAKEWOOD

several bridges in this area

P

P

Windeler Rd.

inset

visitor center

reservoir

HQ

P

P

toll booth

Manasquan Reservoir

Peskin Rd.

© Christopher Mac Kinnon 2003

wildlife observation blind

see inset

cinder path leads to parking lot

entrance

Windeler Rd.

gate

Old Tavern Rd.

dam

bridge

Manassa Rd.

Southard Ave. (to Rte. 524)

FARMINGDALE

MANASQUAN RESERVOIR

TRAIL INFO: This perimeter trail around the shoreline of the Manasquan Reservoir is apx. 5 miles long and can be ridden in either direction. Please stay on the trail. Avoid entering wetland areas, as they are a designated wildlife habitat. This multi-use trail is open to hikers and bikers. A bridge and boardwalk link all sections of the trail. The gravel and dirt surface is suitable for all off-road bicycles. Distance markers are located at mile intervals along the route. The recreation area is open all year round. Hours of operation are posted at the entrance on Windeler Rd. Look for Manasquan Reservoir directional signs on Rte. 9 and I-195.

TRAIL RATING: *easy*
DISTANCE: *apx. 5 miles*
SURFACE: *packed dirt, gravel*

Directions: From I-195, take Exit 28 for Route 9 north toward Freehold. Stay in the right lane on Route 9 and turn right at the 1st traffic light onto Georgia Tavern Road. Follow Georgia Tavern Road for about 0.3 miles and turn right onto Windeler Road. Take Windeler Road for 1.5 miles to the reservoir parking area on the left.

Mercer County Park

Mercer County Park is located about 7 miles southeast of Princeton and 5 miles northeast of Trenton. With approximately 2,500 acres, it is the largest parcel of bike-accessible public land in the Trenton-Mercer County area. This well manicured park boasts a tennis complex, a skating rink, and a marina, as well as picnic areas and lighted softball fields.

Mercer's prominence as a first-class mountain-bike destination has grown in recent years, due primarily to the efforts of SMART (Save Mercer and Ride the Trails). Before this organization got involved, Mercer was a vast complex of unmarked and—for the most part—illegally constructed trails. Mountain biking was at best a tolerated activity.

Since 1999, this group has been instrumental in defining, marking, and maintaining trails at Mercer. Future developments will hopefully include trail brochures and a map describing trail routes.

The route maps for this area show two separate rides, connected by a paved multi-use trail accessible from both the East and West Picnic Area parking lots.

Many miles of flat, winding singletrack through wooded terrain await the off-road enthusiast at Mercer. Trails are letter coded alphabetically and run from A-X. While Mercer's trails can safely be labeled intermediate, they are best avoided after heavy rains, when traction is difficult and erosion to trail surface likely.

Please respect posted no-trespassing signs in the vicinity of the Mercer Oaks Golf Course. This area is off limits to bikes.

Indicated directions are to the West Picnic Area parking. It is approximately 1.75 miles via the paved multi-use trail from the West Picnic Area to the East Picnic Area. The mileage indicated for the Mercer County Park (East) ride (5.1) does not include the 1.75 miles of the paved multi-use trail.

If you prefer to drive to the East Picnic Area, leave the West Picnic Area, turn left onto the park road, and follow it to the stop sign. Turn left on Old Trenton Road. At the first traffic light, turn left. The entrance to the East Picnic Area is on the left about a quarter-mile ahead.

Winter warrior

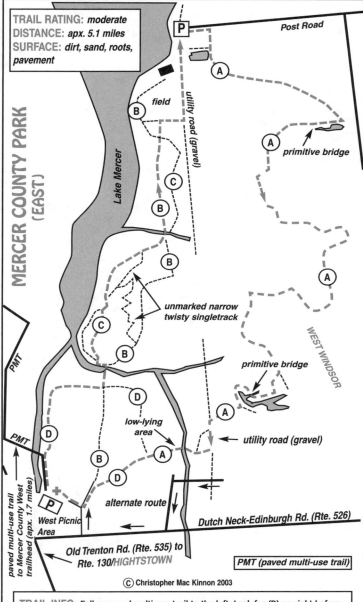

MERCER COUNTY PARK (EAST)

TRAIL RATING: *moderate*
DISTANCE: *apx. 5.1 miles*
SURFACE: *dirt, sand, roots, pavement*

Lake Mercer

field

utility road (gravel)

primitive bridge

unmarked narrow twisty singletrack

WEST WINDSOR

primitive bridge

utility road (gravel)

low-lying area

PMT

PMT

paved multi-use trail to Mercer County West trailhead (apx. 1.7 miles)

West Picnic Area

alternate route

Dutch Neck-Edinburgh Rd. (Rte. 526)

Old Trenton Rd. (Rte. 535) to Rte. 130/HIGHTSTOWN

Post Road

© Christopher Mac Kinnon 2003

PMT (paved multi-use trail)

Directions: From Route I south of Princeton, exit at Quaker Bridge Road (Route 533). Take Quaker Bridge Road south for about 2 miles to Hughes Road. Turn left onto Hughes Road and follow it for about a half mile, turning left onto the main road through Mercer County Park. Follow this road to the West Picnic Area parking lot.

TRAIL INFO: Follow paved multi-use trail to the left. Look for (D) on right before crossing bridge. Follow to 4-way intersection. Go left on (B). Cross primitive bridge. Turn left, then right onto (C). Follow to 3-way intersection. Go left on (B), crossing shallow water. Follow to field. Turn right; follow indistinct trail to gravel utility road. Go left. At parking lot, turn right; follow Post Rd. (paved). About 150 feet ahead, go right on wide doubletrack (A). At pond, it becomes singletrack and goes to left. Follow this remote but obvious singletrack, finally reaching gravel utility road. Turn left. About 150 feet ahead, go right on (A). Pass large pipe to left and ride through low-lying area. At 3-way intersection, go left onto (D). Follow back to parking area. NOTE: Low-lying area is subject to occasional flooding. To bypass this area, continue on gravel past the point where (A) enters woods. At unmarked paved road, go right, crossing pedestrian bridge. Follow to corner. Turn left onto Darvel Rd. Reach Edinburgh Rd. Turn right; follow to park entrance/parking lot.

Mercer County Park
Hughes Road
Hamilton, Lawrence, and West Windsor Townships
Mercer County
609-989-6530

Mercer County Park
Hughes Road
Hamilton, Lawrence,
and West Windsor Townships
Mercer County
609-989-6530

Directions: From Route 1 south of Princeton, exit at Quaker Bridge Road (Route 533). Take Quaker Bridge Road south for 2.2 miles to Hughes Drive. Turn left onto Hughes and follow it for about a half mile, turning left onto the main road through Mercer County Park. Follow this road to the West Picnic Area parking lot.

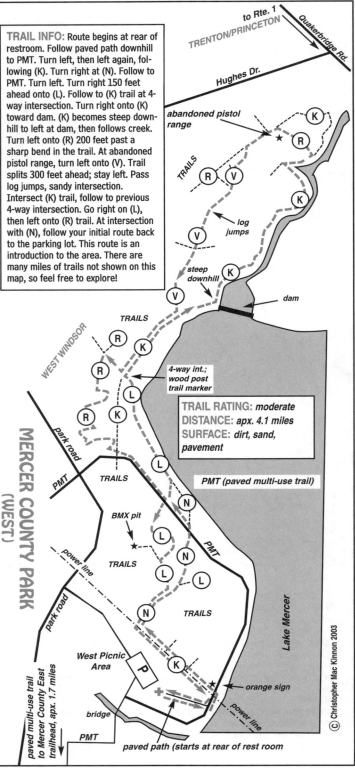

TRAIL INFO: Route begins at rear of restroom. Follow paved path downhill to PMT. Turn left, then left again, following (K). Turn right at (N). Follow to PMT. Turn left. Turn right 150 feet ahead onto (L). Follow to (K) trail at 4-way intersection. Turn right onto (K) toward dam. (K) becomes steep downhill to left at dam, then follows creek. Turn left onto (R) 200 feet past a sharp bend in the trail. At abandoned pistol range, turn left onto (V). Trail splits 300 feet ahead; stay left. Pass log jumps, sandy intersection. Intersect (K) trail, follow to previous 4-way intersection. Go right on (L), then left onto (R) trail. At intersection with (N), follow your initial route back to the parking lot. This route is an introduction to the area. There are many miles of trails not shown on this map, so feel free to explore!

to Rte. 1
TRENTON/PRINCETON
Quakerbridge Rd.
Hughes Dr.

abandoned pistol range

TRAILS

log jumps

steep downhill

dam

WEST WINDSOR

TRAILS

4-way int.; wood post trail marker

TRAIL RATING: *moderate*
DISTANCE: *apx. 4.1 miles*
SURFACE: *dirt, sand, pavement*

park road

PMT

TRAILS

PMT (paved multi-use trail)

MERCER COUNTY PARK (WEST)

BMX pit

TRAILS

power line

park road

TRAILS

Lake Mercer

paved multi-use trail to Mercer County East trailhead, apx. 1.7 miles

West Picnic Area

P

bridge

PMT

power line

orange sign

paved path (starts at rear of rest room

© Christopher Mac Kinnon 2003

Parvin State Park

Parvin State Park in Salem County is a prime multi-use recreation area for residents of South Jersey, and it is one of the few sizable tracts of public land in this part of the state where mountain biking is both appealing and allowed.

Along with swimming, hiking, boating, and horseback riding, bicycling is encouraged by the park. Most trails in the park are well suited for riding. The terrain is generally flat and satisfactory for riders at all levels of ability. Trails vary from wide doubletrack to occasional singletrack, along with several paved sections.

I recommend avoiding the section of the Long Trail (red) between the points where it intersects the Green Trail and where it intersects with a short connector trail. The designated nature trail is located along here and is intended primarily for foot travel. Also, this is a low-lying area that is subject to flooding in wet weather and tends to become overgrown in the warmer months. This area is bypassed by means of the paved park loop road shown on the map.

Be sure to pick up a park brochure before start to ride. It shows the complete network of marked trails and facilities and also provides a wealth of information pertaining to the history of the park.

Several of the trails shown on the route map, as well as numerous intersecting trails, are open to both horses and hikers. Please extend courtesy to both to avoid any unnecessary conflicts. Dismounting in the presence of horses is strongly recommended.

During the summer months, the cool waters of Parvin Lake are available for a refreshing swim. Inquire at the office about access to the beach area.

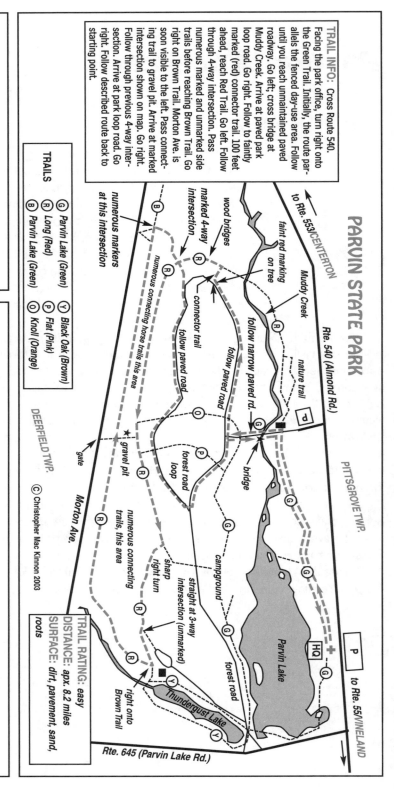

PARVIN STATE PARK

TRAIL INFO: Cross Route 540. Facing the park office, turn right onto the Green Trail. Initially, the route parallels the fenced day-use area. Follow until you reach unmaintained paved roadway. Go left; cross bridge at Muddy Creek. Arrive at park loop road. Go right. Follow to faintly marked (red) connector trail 100 feet ahead, reach Red Trail. Go left. Follow through 4-way intersection. Pass numerous marked and unmarked side trails before reaching Brown Trail. Go right on Brown Trail. Morton Ave. is soon visible to the left. Pass connecting trail to gravel pit. Arrive at marked intersection shown on map. Go right. Follow through previous 4-way intersection. Arrive at park loop road. Go right. Follow described route back to starting point.

TRAILS

Ⓖ	Parvin Lake (Green)	Ⓥ Black Oak (Brown)
Ⓡ	Long (Red)	Ⓟ Flat (Pink)
Ⓑ	Parvin Lake (Green)	Ⓞ Knoll (Orange)

© Christopher Mac Kinnon 2003

DEERFIELD TWP.

PITTSGROVE TWP.

to Rte. 553/CENTERTON

Rte. 540 (Almond Rd.)

to Rte. 55/VINELAND

Muddy Creek

faint red marking on tree

nature trail

follow narrow paved rd.

wood bridges

marked 4-way intersection

connector trail

follow paved road

numerous markers at this intersection

numerous connecting horse trails this area

gate

gravel pit

forest road loop

bridge

campground

straight at 3-way intersection (unmarked)

numerous connecting trails, this area

sharp right turn

forest road

Morton Ave.

right onto Brown Trail

Parvin Lake

Thundergust Lake

Rte. 645 (Parvin Lake Rd.)

TRAIL RATING: easy
DISTANCE: apx. 8.2 miles
SURFACE: dirt, pavement, sand, roots

Parvin State Park
701 Almond Road
Pittsgrove
Salem County
856-358-8616

Directions: From Route 55, take Exit 35 onto Route 674. Follow Route 674 west 2.1 miles to Route 645. Turn left onto Route 645 and follow it 2 miles to Route 540. Turn right onto Route 540. Use the parking lot on the right, across from the park headquarters and Parvin Lake.

Patriots' Path

Patriots' Path is a linear park first envisioned about 20 years ago, when Morris County officials began working on the creation of a continuous multi-use trail connecting parklands as well as recreational and cultural facilities. Foreseeing future development in the area, these far-sighted planners also sought to preserve the land surrounding the Whippany and Raritan Rivers as a buffer between the natural environment and the new construction that would take place.

Today, Patriots' Path is a visible testament to their efforts. The routes shown on the Patriots' Path (East) and Patriots' Path (West) trail maps represent the longest currently developed and bike-accessible portions of this expanding trail. Future plans call for the path to extend as a continuous route from the Lenape Trail in Essex County to Stephens State Park in Hackettstown in Warren County.

Recent trail development includes the addition of the railroad right-of-way through the Black River Wildlife Management Area (see Black River trail map). For Patriots' Path trail updates, refer to current maps posted at the trailhead parking lot (see map), or stop by the Morris County Park Commission office located on Route 24 about a half mile past the entrance to the Lewis Morris County Park.

Patriots' Path could be described as "suburban" in character, especially in the western section. You'll feel in places as if you were riding in someone's backyard—or at least, as is actually the case, right next to it! Since most of Patriots' Path does border on private land, bicyclists should make an effort to stay on the trail. This is a multi-use trail best suited for leisurely riding, and cyclists can expect to encounter both pedestrian and equestrian traffic along the route and should show courtesy to other trail users.

Although classified as "easy" overall, our Patriots' Path (West) route does contain several areas that are subject to erosion damage, as well as a number of small hills that present slightly more difficult riding conditions. There is one steep hill climb about 0.25 miles into the ride along the eastern route. (See trail information box for details.)

Patriots' Path trail marker

Limited parking is available at the trailhead on Route 24 across from Lewis Morris County Park or in the Sunrise Lake parking lot at Lewis Morris (the starting point for the Lewis Morris route; see map for that ride). If you park at Lewis Morris, go past the "No Outlet" sign at the end of the lot. Follow the paved path slowly through the picnic area and you'll find Patriots' Path at the bottom of the hill. Follow it to the right (white blazes) and you'll reach Route 24 and the Patriots' Path parking lot approximately 0.3 miles ahead.

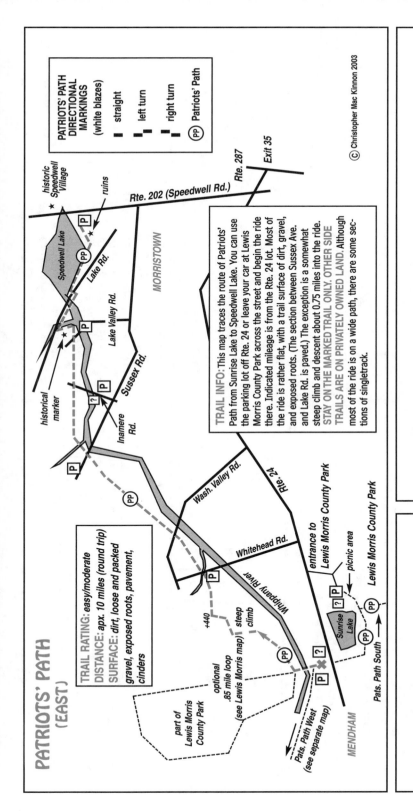

PATRIOTS' PATH (EAST)

PATRIOTS' PATH DIRECTIONAL MARKINGS
(white blazes)

— straight

- - - left turn

- - - right turn

(PP) Patriots' Path

© Christopher Mac Kinnon 2003

historic
Speedwell
Village

ruins

Speedwell Lake

P

(PP)

Lake Rd.

Rte. 202 (Speedwell Rd.)

Rte. 287

Exit 35

MORRISTOWN

historical
marker

P

Lake Valley Rd.

Sussex Rd.

P

?

Inamere
Rd.

P

(PP)

TRAIL INFO: This map traces the route of Patriots' Path from Sunrise Lake to Speedwell Lake. You can use the parking lot off Rte. 24 or leave your car at Lewis Morris County Park across the street and begin the ride there. Indicated mileage is from the Rte. 24 lot. Most of the ride is rather flat, with a trail surface of dirt, gravel, and exposed roots. (The section between Sussex Ave. and Lake Rd. is paved.) The exception is a somewhat steep climb and descent about 0.75 miles into the ride. STAY ON THE MARKED TRAIL ONLY. OTHER SIDE TRAILS ARE ON PRIVATELY OWNED LAND. Although most of the ride is on a wide path, there are some sections of singletrack.

Wash. Valley Rd.

Rte. 24

Whitehead Rd.

entrance to
Lewis Morris County Park

P

picnic area

Lewis Morris County Park

P

?

Sunrise
Lake

(PP)

(PP)

Pats. Path South

TRAIL RATING: *easy/moderate*
DISTANCE: *apx. 10 miles (round trip)*
SURFACE: *dirt, loose and packed gravel, exposed roots, pavement, cinders*

Whippany River

P

+440

steep
climb

(PP)

P

?

X

optional
.85 mile loop
(see Lewis Morris map)

part of
Lewis Morris
County Park

MENDHAM

Pats. Path West
(see separate map)

Patriots' Path
Sunrise Lake to Speedwell Lake
Morris County
973-326-7600

Directions: From I-287, take Exit 35. Follow Route 24 through Morristown (signs may read 24/124). Look for the entrance to Lewis Morris Park on the left and the Patriots' Path parking area on the right, about 3.5 miles west of I-287.

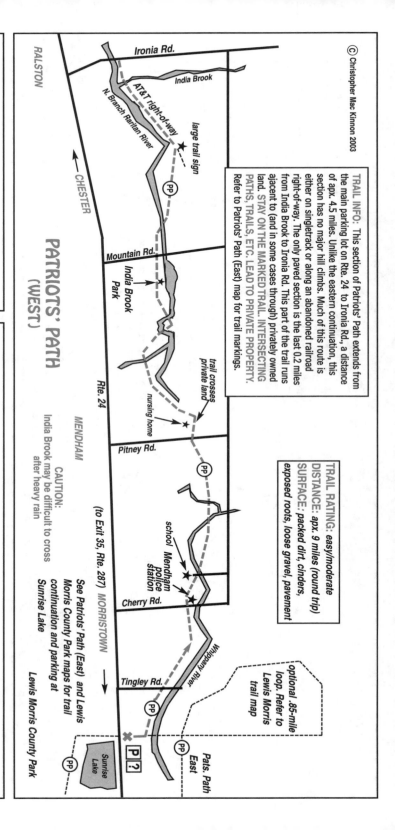

PATRIOTS' PATH
(WEST)

Patriots' Path
Sunrise Lake to Ralston
Morris County
973-326-7600

Directions: From I-287, take Exit 35 (Route 24). Go west on Route 24 through Morristown (signs may read 24/124). Look for the entrance to Lewis Morris Park on the left and the Patriots' Path parking area on the right, about 3.5 miles west of I-287.

TRAIL INFO: This section of Patriots' Path extends from the main parking lot on Rte. 24 to Ironia Rd., a distance of apx. 4.5 miles. Unlike the eastern continuation, this section has no major hill climbs. Much of this route is either on singletrack or along an abandoned railroad right-of-way. The only paved section is the last 0.2 miles from India Brook to Ironia Rd. This part of the trail runs adjacent to (and in some cases through) privately owned land. STAY ON THE MARKED TRAIL. INTERSECTING PATHS, TRAILS, ETC. LEAD TO PRIVATE PROPERTY. Refer to Patriots' Path (East) map for trail markings.

TRAIL RATING: easy/moderate
DISTANCE: apx. 9 miles (round trip)
SURFACE: packed dirt, cinders, exposed roots, loose gravel, pavement

© Christopher Mac Kinnon 2003

Ralston

Ironia Rd.

India Brook

AT&T right-of-way

N. Branch Raritan River

large trail sign

← CHESTER

PP

Mountain Rd.

India Brook Park

trail crosses private land

nursing home

Rte. 24

MENDHAM

CAUTION:
India Brook may be difficult to cross after heavy rain

Pitney Rd.

PP

(to Exit 35, Rte. 287) MORRISTOWN →

school

Mendham police station

Cherry Rd.

Whippany River

Tingley Rd.

PP

PP

See Patriots' Path (East) and Lewis Morris County Park maps for trail continuation and parking at Sunrise Lake

Sunrise Lake

Lewis Morris County Park

P ?

PP

Pats Path East

optional .85-mile loop. Refer to Lewis Morris trail map

Paulinskill Valley Rail Trail

 Scenery and serenity abound along this ribbon of rail trail that snakes its way through rural Warren and Sussex Counties. This is a New Jersey devoid of strip malls and suburban sprawl.

While the hard-core rider may opt to ride the entire described route (approximately 49 miles) in one day, we've broken the trail down into two sections, east and west, for those less ambitious. This allows the leisurely or recreational rider to complete either section without difficulty. Generally speaking, this is a lightly used trail in comparison with the Delaware and Raritan Canal, the only other off-road ride in New Jersey of comparable length.

Footbridge Park in Blairstown appears to be the unofficial "hub" for rail-trail traffic, in all likelihood because of its large parking area, its proximity to Route 94, and, of course, the park itself. Even here, trail use on weekends is moderate at worst. Unlike the Sussex Branch Rail Trail, which intersects quite a few ridable singletrack trails, the Paulinskill requires riders to remain on the trail. Most of the surrounding land is either posted or obviously private.

A side trip to Swartswood State Park via road travel is possible. There are several trails of moderate difficulty open to mountain biking at Swartswood. Inquire at the park office or call ahead (973-383-5230) for current trail conditions.

To get to Swartswood from the Paulinskill Trail: At the intersection of the Paulinskill Trail and Route 622 (on the eastern trail map), go left, follow the road over Paulinskill Lake, and continue for about 1.5 miles to Swartswood State Park. Follow signs to the park office.

The Paulinskill follows a railbed last used as a working railroad in 1963. For most of its length, its surface of cinders and dirt is conducive to all but road bikes. Expect some minor trail erosion between Cedar Ridge Road and Henfoot Road (in the western section), as well as some slightly overgrown stretches as you near the eastern terminus of the trail near Sparta Junction (in the eastern section).

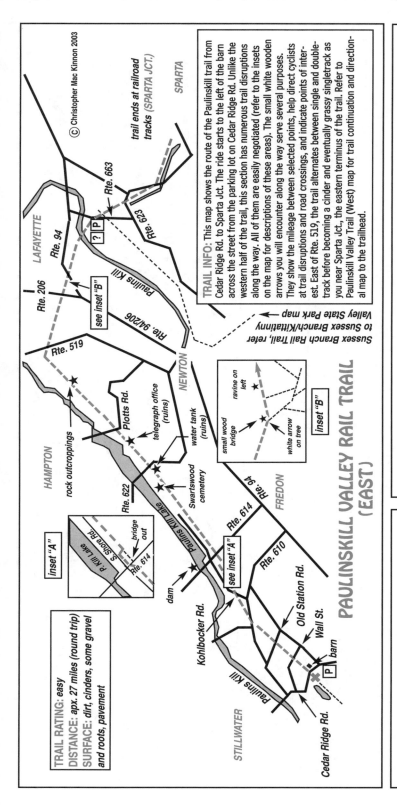

TRAIL RATING: easy
DISTANCE: apx. 27 miles (round trip)
SURFACE: dirt, cinders, some gravel and roots, pavement

TRAIL INFO: This map shows the route of the Paulinskill trail from Cedar Ridge Rd. to Sparta Jct. The ride starts to the left of the barn across the street from the parking lot on Cedar Ridge Rd. Unlike the western half of the trail, this section has numerous trail disruptions along the way. All of them are easily negotiated (refer to the insets on the map for descriptions of these areas). The small white wooden arrows you will encounter along the way serve several purposes. They show the mileage between selected points, help direct cyclists at trail disruptions and road crossings, and indicate points of interest. East of Rte. 519, the trail alternates between single and double-track before becoming a cinder and eventually grassy singletrack as you near Sparta Jct, the eastern terminus of the trail. Refer to Paulinskill Valley Trail (West) map for trail continuation and directional map to the trailhead.

Sussex Branch Trail, refer to Sussex Branch/Kittatinny Valley State Park map

PAULINSKILL VALLEY RAIL TRAIL (EAST)

Directions: From I-80, get off at Exit 12 and take Route 521 north to Blairstown. Make a right onto Route 94 north and follow it for about 6.75 miles. Turn left onto Fairview Hill Road, then right onto Fredon Marksboro Road, then left onto Dixon Road. The parking area is at the bottom of the hill next to a pond.

Paulinskill Valley Rail Trail
Knowlton Township
to Sparta Junction
Warren and Sussex Counties
973-786-6445

© Christopher Mac Kinnon 2003

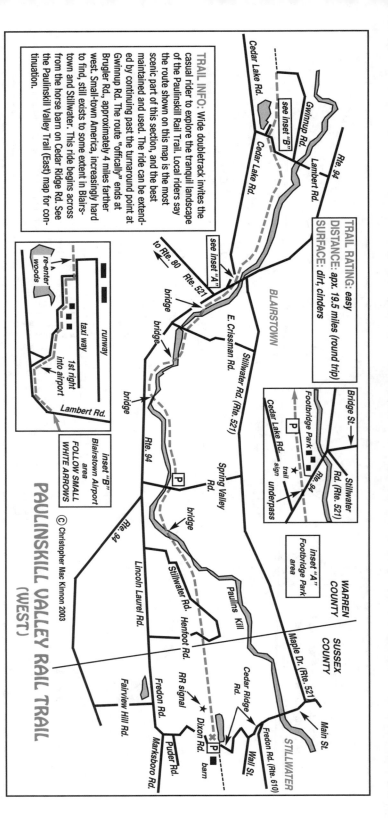

Paulinskill Valley Rail Trail
Knowlton Township
to Sparta Junction
Warren and Sussex Counties
973-786-6445

TRAIL INFO: Wide doubletrack invites the casual rider to explore the tranquil landscape of the Paulinskill Rail Trail. Local riders say the route shown on this map is the most scenic part of this section, and the best maintained and used. The ride can be extended by continuing past the turnaround point at Gwinnup Rd. The route "officially" ends at Brugler Rd., approximately 4 miles farther west. Small-town America, increasingly hard to find, still exists to some extent in Blairstown and Stillwater. This ride begins across from the horse barn on Cedar Ridge Rd. See the Paulinskill Valley Trail (East) map for continuation.

TRAIL RATING: easy
DISTANCE: apx. 19.5 miles (round trip)
SURFACE: dirt, cinders

© Christopher Mac Kinnon 2003

PAULINSKILL VALLEY RAIL TRAIL
(WEST)

Cedar Lake Rd.
Gwinnup Rd.
Lambert Rd.
Rte. 94
Cedar Lake Rd.
see inset "B"

see inset "A"
to Rte. 80
Rte. 521
bridge
bridge
BLAIRSTOWN
E. Crissman Rd.
Stillwater Rd. (Rte. 521)

WARREN COUNTY
SUSSEX COUNTY

Bridge St.
Footbridge Park
Cedar Lake Rd.
Stillwater Rd. (Rte. 521)
P
trail sign
underpass
inset "A"
Footbridge Park area

Main St.
Maple Dr. (Rte. 521)
STILLWATER
Fredon Rd. (Rte. 610)
Wall St.
Cedar Ridge Rd.
RR signal
Dixon Rd.
P
barn
Puder Rd.
Fredon Rd.
Marksboro Rd.
Fairview Hill Rd.
Henfoot Rd.
Stillwater Rd.
Lincoln Laurel Rd.
bridge
Spring Valley Rd.
Rte. 94
P
Rte. 94
Paulins Kill

re-enter woods
runway
taxi way
1st right into airport
Lambert Rd.
inset "B"
Blairstown Airport area
FOLLOW SMALL
WHITE ARROWS

Directions: From I-80, get off at Exit 12 and take Route 521 north to Blairstown. Make a right onto Route 94 north and follow it for about 6.75 miles. Turn left onto Fairview Hill Road, then right onto Fredon Marksboro Road, then left onto Dixon Road. The parking area is at the bottom of the hill next to a pond.

Ringwood State Park

At 5,000 plus acres, Ringwood State Park is one of the larger tracts of public land in northeastern New Jersey. The fact that it can be described as "mountain-bike friendly" makes it even more attractive as an off-road cycling destination.

In addition to the described route, many other trails are available for riding. Among these is the rugged singletrack racecourse maintained by a local cycling club. At most marked trail intersections, trail usage and availability will be indicated. Look for brown markers with symbols indicating which activities are allowed on the respective trail. Please keep in mind that both trail usage and permitted activities are subject to change or revision.

The English country-style mansion Skylands Manor, located in the northern section of the park, is modeled after an English estate home of 400 years ago. Tours are available here and at the park's other country house, called Ringwood Manor. You can stop at the park office for detailed information about the park's facilities.

The New Jersey State Botanical Gardens occupy approximately 1,100 acres of the park. Although part of the described route passes through this area, cyclists must stay on the paved road indicated on the map. Off-road riding is strictly forbidden in this area.

Seasonal hunting, swimming, and boating are among other recreational opportunities at Ringwood.

© Christopher Mac Kinnon 2003

Ringwood State Park
Sloatswood Road
Ringwood
Passaic County
973-962-7031

Directions: From Route 287, take Exit 57 and follow signs to Ringwood State Park. Use parking lot "C" in Skylands area off Morris Road.

Shepherd Lake

Potake Pond

follow road through gates

P

?

★

trail parallels shoreline

pipeline

follow park road

left at fork

Morris Rd.

to park headquarters

Sloatsburg Rd.

inset

to Glasmere Ponds

this way first

large boulder

guardrail

to Rte. 511

BOTANICAL GARDENS

4-way int.; cont. straight

metal sign on tree

straight at 3-way int.

pipe

left uphill

numerous trails to the right; continue straight

metal sign on tree

go past stone pillars (keep left) ★

ruins

Pipeline

green trail marker

Glasmere Ponds

G

evergreens

see inset

left at 3-way int.

B

long uphill

B

W

? P

parking lot "C"

W

cross white trail

large boulder

Weyble Pond

W

R

Honeysuckle La.

one way

exit road

keep left

W

W

W

white trail goes right; cont. straight; follow blue blazes

turn right at white birch trees; follow white trail uphill

TRAILS
Ⓡ Red trail
Ⓑ Blue trail
Ⓦ White trail
Ⓖ Green trail

go past yellow gate; follow wide middle road

small stone bridge

grass field

W

Brushwood Pond

numerous unmarked trails on right

boulders

TRAIL RATING: *moderate*
DISTANCE: *apx. 11.0 miles*
SURFACE: *rocky eroded fire and carriage roads, pavement*

TRAIL INFO: This ride through Ringwood State Park uses the extensive network of doubletrack carriage and fire roads along with sections of paved park road. Despite the rugged terrain, the route enables you to explore the backcountry of Ringwood while avoiding some of the more difficult trails. (There is one long hill climb about halfway through the ride.) Challenging singletrack along with a marked route maintained by the Ramapo Mountain Bike Club offer additional possibilities for riding. Many intersections have posted markers indicating whether the trails can be used by hikers, bikers, or equestrians. The park is also well known for its impressive botanical gardens and historic buildings. To reach the trailhead, follow Morris Rd. to the Skylands entrance area. Proceed to lot "C," following posted signs. As you head out of lot "C" on your bike, bear to the left on the paved road leading slightly downhill. (Do not go hard left against one-way traffic, or right, the way you came in.) DO NOT RIDE ON TRAILS DESIGNATED FOR HIKING ONLY!

RINGWOOD STATE PARK

Notes:

Cushetunk Trail sign

Round Valley Recreation Area

Your first impression of the Round Valley Recreation Area will be of size. Large by New Jersey standards, the reservoir and horseshoe-shaped Cushetunk Mountain dwarf many of the other ride locations in this book. Round Valley is big not only in physical size (with a combined 7,300-plus acres) but psychologically as well, perhaps because of the configuration of the surrounding mountains and expanse of pristine water.

Regarded as the mecca of New Jersey mountain biking by some, its reputation is well deserved. You can expect both conditioning and bike-handling skills to be tested here.

This out-and-back route starts off innocently enough as a relatively tame trail heading away from the parking lot. It doesn't really begin to reveal its true identity until about 1.5 miles into the ride. After reaching a chain-link fence, the trail descends steeply, the first of many steep climbs and descents. From this point on, you can expect to encounter long and demanding ascents and descents, as well as heavily eroded sections of trail and rocks the size of bowling balls.

An equipment check is a must at Round Valley. Stock up on extra tubes, patches, etc. before starting out. This is a punishing ride where self-reliance is the rule. For emergency purposes there's a telephone located at the beach area next to a small cluster of buildings at approximately 5.6 miles into the route (see trail map).

Round Valley is a multi-use recreation area. Although it serves primarily as a water source holding in excess of 50 billion gallons, it is also highly valued by fisherman, boaters, and hikers. Cyclists should ride slowly in the area near the wilderness parking area. This section of the trail is heavily used by pedestrians who want to view the reservoir. The nearby Pine Tree Trail is off limits to bikes. Stay on the designated route (the Cushetunk Trail) and watch for posted private-property signs to the right as you ride the prescribed route. This trail is marked with various symbols including a horseshoe, footprint, and arrow, as shown in the trail sign pictured at left.

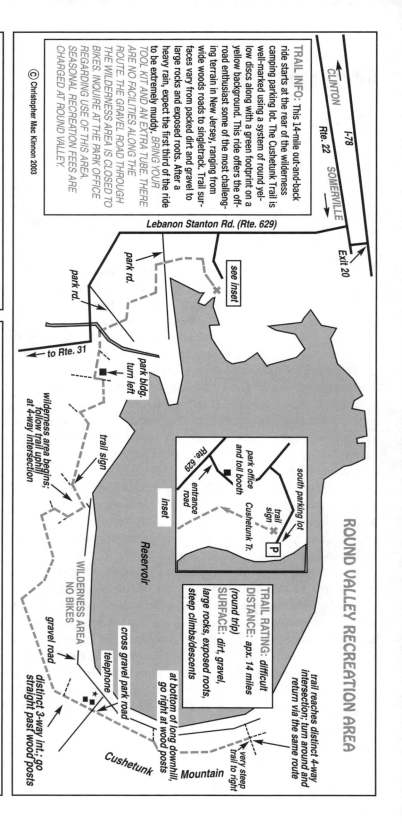

Round Valley Recreation Area
Route 629 (Lebanon-Stanton Road)
Lebanon
Hunterdon County
908-236-6355

Directions: Take I-78 to Exit 20 and follow signs to Round Valley Recreation Area via Route 22, parking at the entrance off Route 629 (Lebanon-Stanton Road).

TRAIL INFO: This 14-mile out-and-back ride starts at the rear of the wilderness camping parking lot. The Cushetunk Trail is well-marked using a system of round yellow discs along with a green footprint on a yellow background. This ride offers the off-road enthusiast some of the most challenging terrain in New Jersey, ranging from wide woods roads to singletrack. Trail surfaces vary from packed dirt and gravel to large rocks and exposed roots. After a heavy rain, expect the first third of the ride to be extremely muddy. *BRING YOUR TOOL KIT AND AN EXTRA TUBE. THERE ARE NO FACILITIES ALONG THIS ROUTE. THE GRAVEL ROAD THROUGH THE WILDERNESS AREA IS CLOSED TO BIKES. INQUIRE AT THE PARK OFFICE REGARDING USE OF THIS AREA. SEASONAL RECREATION FEES ARE CHARGED AT ROUND VALLEY.*

© Christopher Mac Kinnon 2003

I-78
Rte. 22
CLINTON
SOMERVILLE
Exit 20

Lebanon Stanton Rd. (Rte. 629)

park rd.
see inset
to Rte. 31
park bldg.
turn left
trail sign
wilderness area begins;
follow trail uphill
at 4-way intersection

ROUND VALLEY RECREATION AREA

inset
Rte. 629
park office
and toll booth
entrance
road
trail
sign
Cushetunk Tr.
south parking lot
P

Reservoir

WILDERNESS AREA
NO BIKES

gravel road
cross gravel park road
telephone
distinct 3-way int.; go
straight past wood posts

at bottom of long downhill,
go right at wood posts

Cushetunk
Mountain

very steep
trail to right

trail reaches distinct 4-way
intersection; turn around and
return via the same route

TRAIL RATING: difficult
DISTANCE: apx. 14 miles
(round trip)
SURFACE: dirt, gravel,
large rocks, exposed roots,
steep climbs/descents

Shark River County Park

Located on the border of Wall and Neptune Townships in southern Monmouth County, Shark River Park is easily accessible from the Garden State Parkway or Routes 34 and 18. At 588 acres, it is one of the mid-size parks within the Monmouth County Park System. In addition to cycling, Shark River offers opportunities for fishing and hiking, and it includes a playground and a fitness trail.

Though not as well known as other Monmouth County destinations such as Hartshorne or Huber Woods, this park offers trails that are best suited for novice to moderately skilled riders. It is the perfect destination for the cyclist wanting to venture onto singletrack trail without having to deal with a multitude of trail obstacles.

Most of this route uses the park's network of hard-packed, wide, flat to rolling woods paths. For lack of a better description, they are referred to as "trails," both on the posted map at the trailhead and on our route map of the area.

Despite its proximity to both the Garden State Parkway and the surrounding neighborhoods, this ride includes areas where you will experience the feeling of being in a remote wooded area.

The Hidden Creek Trail is marked as multi-use. Stay alert on the singletrack portions of this trail. There are several short trails on the other side of Schoolhouse Road. This is the primary day-use area of the park and as a result it is sometimes quite congested, so it is best avoided by cyclists.

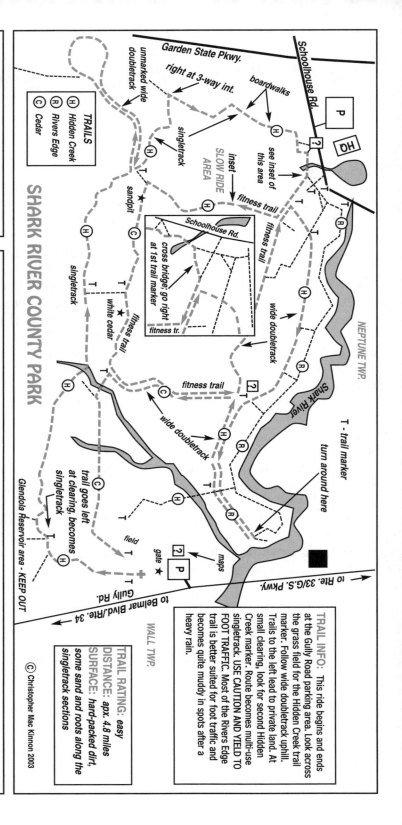

Shark River County Park
Schoolhouse Road
Wall and Neptune Townships
Monmouth County
732-842-4000

Directions: From the Garden State Parkway, take Exit 100. Go east on Route 33 about 0.7 miles to Gully Road. Turn right onto Gully and follow it to the parking lot about 0.7 miles ahead on right.

SHARK RIVER COUNTY PARK

TRAILS
Ⓗ Hidden Creek
Ⓡ Rivers Edge
Ⓒ Cedar

T - trail marker

NEPTUNE TWP.

WALL TWP.

TRAIL INFO: This ride begins and ends at the Gully Road parking area. Look across the grass field for the Hidden Creek trail marker. Follow wide doubletrack uphill. Trails to the left lead to private land. At small clearing, look for second Hidden Creek marker. Route becomes multi-use singletrack. USE CAUTION AND YIELD TO FOOT TRAFFIC. Most of the Rivers Edge trail is better suited for foot traffic and becomes quite muddy in spots after a heavy rain.

TRAIL RATING: easy
DISTANCE: apx. 4.8 miles
SURFACE: hard-packed dirt, some sand and roots along the singletrack sections

© Christopher Mac Kinnon 2003

to Belmar Blvd./Rte. 34
to Rte. 33/G.S. Pkwy.
Gully Rd.
Glendola Reservoir area - KEEP OUT

Garden State Pkwy.
Schoolhouse Rd.
Shark River

Six Mile Run Reservoir

The first thing you'll probably ask yourself as you start this ride is "where's the reservoir?"

The answer is "right here" and "there really isn't one … yet."

Confusing? Not really. According to the park brochure, development of this project won't begin until around the year 2020, giving cyclists ample time to explore this hidden off-road resource in central New Jersey.

In an earlier era, the area was cultivated by Dutch farmers who had migrated from Long Island, and many barns here date back to this time. Preserved today as a multi-use recreation area (seasonal bow hunting is permitted) and watershed, it stands as a visual reminder of an agrarian landscape once common in the Raritan Valley area.

In contrast to the nearby Delaware and Raritan Canal towpath, which is quite flat, this route uses rolling doubletrack (watch out for the groundhog holes!) as well as narrow singletrack with occasional trail obstacles and possible shallow water crossings.

Perhaps the word "potential" best describes Six Mile Run. Although the facility is sizable at 3,000 acres, only sections of this site are now open to the public. Cyclists should not cross Six Mile Run, as the area south of the creek is currently closed to bikes. This may or may not change at some future date, according to park personnel, who also report that both trail designations and trail routes are subject to change pending further assessment of activity requirements and environmental impact. Because of this, it would be a good idea to inquire at the park office regarding current trail conditions and updates before starting your ride.

The route shown on this map uses the yellow-blazed singletrack trail, which runs adjacent to Six Mile Run, and a section of the blue-blazed North Pilot Trail. This short ride is intended to be an introduction to this area rather than an attempt at a comprehensive tour through the entire site. For information on the nearby towpath trail and roads in the area, refer to the Delaware and Raritan Canal (South) map.

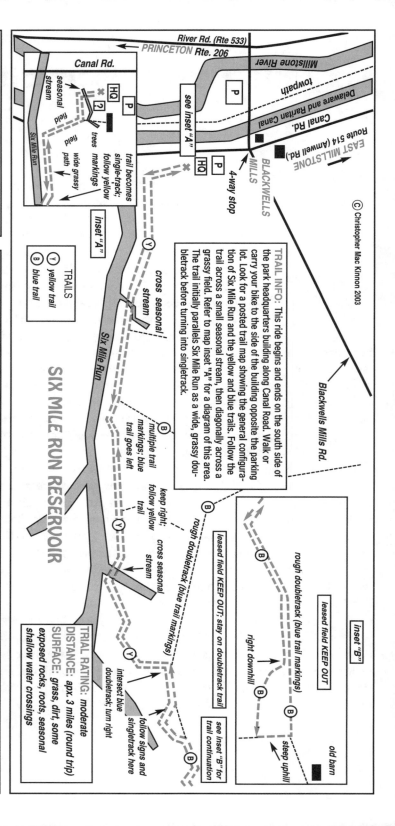

Six Mile Run Reservoir
Canal Road
Blackwells Mills
Somerset County
732-873-3050

© Christopher Mac Kinnon 2003

Blackwells Mills Rd.

PRINCETON Rte. 206

River Rd. (Rte 533)

Millstone River

Delaware and Raritan Canal towpath

Canal Rd.

Route 514 (Amwell Rd.)

EAST MILLSTONE

BLACKWELLS MILLS

4-way stop

see inset "A"

P · HQ · P

inset "A"

Canal Rd.

seasonal/ stream

field

field

trees

HQ

?

single-track; follow yellow markings

trail becomes

wide grassy path

Six Mile Run

TRAILS
Ⓨ yellow trail
Ⓑ blue trail

TRAIL INFO: This ride begins and ends on the south side of the park headquarters building along Canal Road. Walk or carry your bike to the side of the building opposite the parking lot. Look for a posted trail map showing the general configuration of Six Mile Run and the yellow and blue trails. Follow the trail across a small seasonal stream, then diagonally across a grassy field. Refer to map inset "A" for a diagram of this area. The trail initially parallels Six Mile Run as a wide, grassy doubletrack before turning into singletrack.

SIX MILE RUN RESERVOIR

Six Mile Run

Ⓨ cross seasonal stream

Ⓑ multiple trail markings; blue trail goes left

Ⓑ rough doubletrack (blue trail markings)

Ⓨ keep right; follow yellow trail

cross seasonal stream

Ⓑ leased field KEEP OUT; stay on doubletrack trail

inset "B"

leased field KEEP OUT

rough doubletrack (blue trail markings)

Ⓑ

Ⓑ right downhill

Ⓑ

Ⓑ see inset "B" for trail continuation

Ⓑ steep uphill

old barn

Ⓨ intersect blue doubletrack; turn right

follow signs and singletrack here

TRIAL RATING: moderate
DISTANCE: apx. 3 miles (round trip)
SURFACE: grass, dirt, some exposed rocks, roots, seasonal shallow water crossings

see inset "A"

Directions: From Route 206 in Hillsborough, go east on Route 514 (Amwell Road). In Millstone, turn right onto Route 533 (Millstone River Road). Go south 2.1 miles, turn left onto Blackwells Mills Road, and cross the canal bridge. Turn right onto Canal Road and park near the Delaware and Raritan Canal headquarters building, which is the second structure on the left. Parking for this ride is also available at the large lot between the Millstone River and the canal. To reach this area, cross over the canal at the 4-way stop just north of the park headquarters entrance (see map for location).

Stokes State Forest

The present-day Stokes State Forest, with land holdings in excess of 15,000 acres, began as a 500-acre land donation by former Gov. Edward C. Stokes, who served from 1905 to 1908. Today Stokes and nearby High Point State Park, which can be reached via a connecting trail, offer a combined total of approximately 30,000 acres, most of which is accessible to mountain bikers.

The Parker Trail, which links the two areas, is shown on the High Point and Stokes trail maps. Camping is available at either park, which is convenient for hard-core riders looking for two continuous days of serious riding.

Stokes is similar to High Point in terrain and trail composition, and trails at Stokes are also lightly traveled. Most of the traffic you will encounter, whether in the form of cars, hikers, or other cyclists, will be in the vicinity of scenic Sunrise Mountain and along Kittle Road, a popular day-use area.

This entire route lies within the section of Stokes Forest that is northeast of Route 206. For information regarding trail availability southwest of Route 206, stop by the park headquarters near the trailhead.

One feature of the southern section of the park is Tillman Ravine, a natural area of small waterfalls, rock outcroppings, and hemlocks. It is off limits to bikes, but certainly worthy of exploration by foot. (Refer to park-issued map for location.)

The Tinsley Geological Trail (see map) features sections of adjoining terrain that illustrate the effects of glacial movement. You can get more information on this trail at the park headquarters.

Stokes' extensive network of trails and structures is the direct result of Civilian Conservation Corps efforts during the 1930s. They endure today as multi-use trails and facilities.

Seasonal boating, fishing, and picnicking are popular activities at Stokes State Forest.

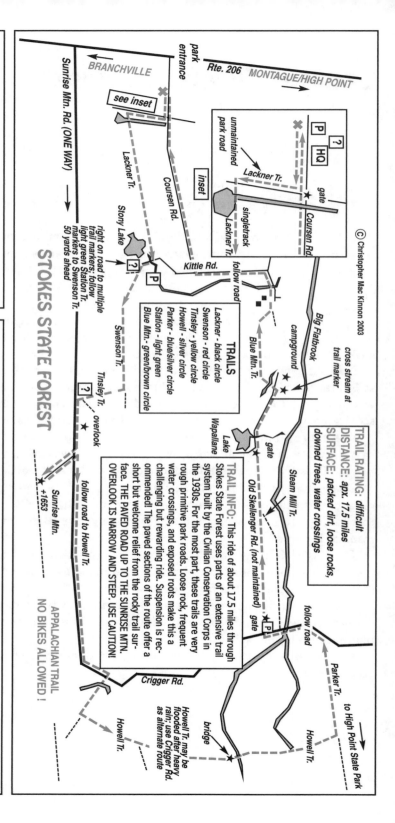

Stokes State Forest
Coursen Road
Branchville
Sussex County
973-948-3820

Directions: From Route 80, take Exit 25 and follow Route 206 north approximately 20 miles to Branchville. Continue north on Route 206 past Culvers Lake on the right. Go through Culvers Gap and pass Sunrise Mountain Road on the right. Park at the Stokes State Forest office, ahead on the right.

© Christopher Mac Kinnon 2003

STOKES STATE FOREST

Rte. 206 MONTAGUE/HIGH POINT →

BRANCHVILLE ←

park entrance

Sunrise Mtn. Rd. (ONE WAY) →

see inset

Coursen Rd.

Lackner Tr.

inset

unmaintained park road

P HQ ?

Lackner Tr.

gate

singletrack

Lackner Tr.

Coursen Rd.

cross stream at trail marker

Big Flatbrook

campground

Blue Mtn. Tr.

Steam Mill Tr.

follow road

Kittle Rd.

Story Lake

?

P

TRAILS
Lackner - black circle
Swenson - red circle
Tinsley - yellow circle
Howell - silver circle
Parker - blue/silver circle
Station - light green
Blue Mtn.- green/brown circle

right on road to multiple trail markers; follow light green Station Tr. markers to Swenson Tr. 50 yards ahead

Swenson Tr.

Tinsley Tr.

?

overlook

Lake Wapaliane

gate

Old Skellenger Rd. (not maintained) gate

P

TRAIL INFO: This ride of about 17.5 miles through Stokes State Forest uses parts of an extensive trail system built by the Civilian Conservation Corps in the 1930s. For the most part, these trails are very rough primitive park roads. Loose rock, frequent water crossings, and exposed roots make this a challenging but rewarding ride. Suspension is recommended! The paved sections of the route offer a short but welcome relief from the rocky trail surface. THE PAVED ROAD UP TO THE SUNRISE MTN. OVERLOOK IS NARROW AND STEEP. USE CAUTION!

follow road

Parker Tr.

to High Point State Park →

Howell Tr.

bridge

Howell Tr. may be flooded after heavy rain; use Crigger Rd. as alternate route

Crigger Rd.

Howell Tr.

APPALACHIAN TRAIL
NO BIKES ALLOWED !

Sunrise Mtn. +1653

follow road to Howell Tr.

TRAIL RATING: difficult
DISTANCE: apx. 17.5 miles
SURFACE: packed dirt, loose rocks, downed trees, water crossings

Sussex Branch/ Kittatinny Valley State Park

This ride through the countryside of rural Sussex County combines a portion of the Sussex Branch Rail Trail with a loop through adjoining Kittatinny Valley State Park. The Sussex Branch is similar in some respects to the Paulinskill Valley Rail Trail, but it runs largely adjacent to or through state-owned parkland, while the Paulinskill borders private land for most of its length.

Beginning at its southern terminus, the Sussex Branch passes through a section of Allamuchy Mountain State Park as a wide cinder/dirt path before appearing to end after about 2 miles. (For information on the location of this section of trail, refer to the Allamuchy Mountain State Park map.)

Unfortunately, the Sussex Branch Rail Trail consists of several unconnected sections. In some areas the trail is maintained, while other segments are overgrown. Current park-issued trail maps reflect the numerous interruptions that prevent it from being a truly continuous route. However, after the trail crosses Route 206 north of Andover, where this ride begins and ends, it continues as an interrupted trail until reaching Route 616 south of Newton, the turnaround point.

From the trailhead next to Route 206, follow the route northward as it passes through Kittatinny Valley State Park. There are many opportunities to explore the intersecting side trails you will encounter here.

Caution: Watch for posted private property signs to the left of the trail before reaching Goodale Road.

Twin Lakes and its associated property were purchased in 1997, and the area is now open for use. Singletrack trails are available for exploration.

When you reach Route 616 south of Newton, turn around and retrace your route to the point where you see a stone wall/gate that you had previously passed. Go through the gate and follow the dirt road (see map for trail continuation through Kittatinny Valley State Park). The landscape of Kittatinny is a microcosm of rural Sussex County, featuring dense forest, tranquil meadows, and rugged rock outcroppings. Kittatinny State Park was once a privately owned estate/airport, which was acquired by the state of New Jersey in 1994.

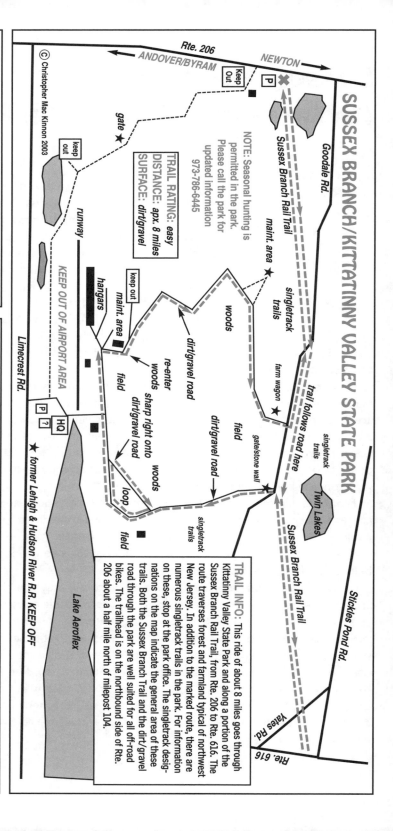

SUSSEX BRANCH/KITTATINNY VALLEY STATE PARK

Rte. 206

ANDOVER/BYRAM

NEWTON →

Goodale Rd.

Keep Out

P ✕

Sussex Branch Rail Trail

maint. area

NOTE: Seasonal hunting is permitted in the park. Please call the park for updated information 973-786-6445

TRAIL RATING: *easy*
DISTANCE: *apx. 8 miles*
SURFACE: *dirt/gravel*

© Christopher Mac Kinnon 2003

gate ★

keep out

singletrack trails

woods

farm wagon ★

trail follows road here

singletrack trails

Twin Lakes

Stickles Pond Rd.

runway

KEEP OUT OF AIRPORT AREA

hangars

keep out

maint. area

dirt/gravel road

re-enter woods

field

dirt/gravel road

field

gate/stone wall

Limecrest Rd.

P ? HQ

sharp right onto woods

loop

field

singletrack trails

★ former Lehigh & Hudson River R.R. KEEP OFF

Lake Aeroflex

Yates Rd.

Rte. 616

TRAIL INFO: This ride of about 8 miles goes through Kittatinny Valley State Park and along a portion of the Sussex Branch Rail Trail, from Rte. 206 to Rte. 616. The route traverses forest and farmland typical of northwest New Jersey. In addition to the marked route, there are numerous singletrack trails in the park. For information on these, stop at the park office. The singletrack designations on the map indicate the general area of these trails. Both the Sussex Branch Trail and the dirt/gravel road through the park are well suited for all off-road bikes. The trailhead is on the northbound side of Rte. 206 about a half mile north of milepost 104.

Kittatinny Valley State Park
off Route 669 (Limecrest Road)
Andover
Sussex County
973-786-6445

Directions: From Route 80, take Exit 25 and follow Route 206 north approximately 7 miles through Andover. Continue north on Route 206 past Limecrest Road. Look for a Sussex Branch Trail sign and dirt parking area on the right.

Tatum County Park

This 3.8-mile ride through Tatum County Park may be relatively short, but its combination of open fields and secluded singletrack make a pleasant outing for the intermediate rider.

The route uses two of the park's multi-use trails, Tatum Ramble and Meadow Run. Both are indicated by blue square markings. The park's rolling terrain of woodland and fields is accessible by a number of trails and dirt roads, but riders should note that the Holly Grove Trail, the Dogwood Trail, and portions of the Indian Springs Trail are all closed to bicycle traffic.

The property that is Tatum Park today was purchased in 1905 by Charles Tatum of New York City, a manufacturer of commercial glassware. The fields that are part of the described route were first cleared and cultivated around 1920. A donation of 75 acres in 1975 by a member of the Tatum family marked the beginning of what is now Tatum Park, which is part of the Monmouth County Park System.

Subsequent purchases over the years increased the park to its present size of 368 acres. The Holland Activity Center, located next to the parking lot, is home to the Monmouth Conservation Foundation, a group instrumental in land acquisition for preservation in Monmouth County.

A 5-minute drive to the Red Hill Activity Center located off Red Hill Road is a good way to extend your day's outing to Tatum Park. Here you will find the Holly Grove Trail, a short, half-mile loop through a magnificent grove of holly trees (foot traffic only). Across from the Red Hill Activity Center parking area is the entrance to Deep Cut Gardens, a county-owned horticultural masterpiece, dedicated to the home gardener.

To reach this area, turn right onto Van Schoick Road after exiting the park. At the first intersection, turn right onto Holland Road. (Don't try to bike to this area, because Red Hill Road is narrow, with many blind curves.)

TRAIL INFO: Follow grassy trail downhill, crossing dirt road and pedestrian bridge. Short steep uphill leads to field. Trail runs through middle of field, continuing to the point where it initially enters woods. Follow wide path, which becomes singletrack. Reach dirt road at trail marker, now following Meadow Run. Trail continues as singletrack before reaching first of several fields. Follow perimeter of fields (see map). Cross dirt road with gate visible to right. Continue around field, eventually passing trail marker as route enters woods. Follow dirt road to the point where road ends. Make right onto unmarked singletrack. Follow to dirt road; turn right. You will soon come to the point where you initially entered the woods. From here, retrace your route back to the parking lot.

© *Christopher Mac Kinnon 2003*

Directions: From the Garden State Parkway, take Exit 114. Go east on Red Hill Road and continue to Van Schoick Road, about a quarter of a mile ahead. Turn left onto Van Schoick and go about a mile to Holland Road. Turn right onto Holland and follow it to the parking lot on the right.

Red Hill Rd.

to Exit 114/Garden State Parkway

enter woods

enter woods; primitive road becomes singletrack

right onto singletrack (no sign)

gate

dirt road

dirt road

dirt road

MIDDLETOWN

field

field

field

field

field

field

exit woods; keep right

T - trail marker

dirt road

field

field

bridge, steep uphill

TRAILS

(T) *Tatum Rumble (blue)*

(M) *Meadow Run (blue)*

TRAIL RATING: *moderate*
DISTANCE: *apx. 3.8 miles*
SURFACE: *dirt, grass, sand*

?

P

Holland Activity Center

Holland Rd.

Van Schoick Rd.

to Exit 114/Garden State Parkway

← to Red Hill Rd.

TATUM COUNTY PARK

Voorhees State Park

The beginnings of Voorhees State Park can be traced back to 1929, when Foster M. Voorhees, a former governor of New Jersey, donated his 325-acre farm to the people of the state. Succeeding land acquisitions have increased the size of the park to its present 640 acres.

Trails, shelters, and picnic sites were constructed during the 1930s under the Civilian Conservation Corps. Since that time, Voorhees has grown into a multi-use facility. In addition to mountain biking, fishing, hunting, and hiking are among the activities available at the park. Trails here are multi-use except for the Cross Park Trail, which is restricted to foot travel only. The Highland Trail, which is not indicated on the park trail map, also runs through the park. This is a relatively new trail connecting parks, forests, and public open spaces in northern New Jersey and southern New York State. It is advisable to check at the park office regarding access to this trail.

One of the outstanding features of the park is the observatory located off Hill Acres Road (see the map for location). The 28-inch reflector telescope is one of the largest privately owned telescopes in the state. The New Jersey Astronomical Association offers various programs throughout the year. For information, call 908-638-8500.

This loop ride through the park uses wide doubletrack trails, primitive park roads, paved road, and a short stretch of singletrack on the section of trail between the observatory and the scenic overlook. Keep an eye out for hikers who may be using this route to walk from the overlook area to the observatory.

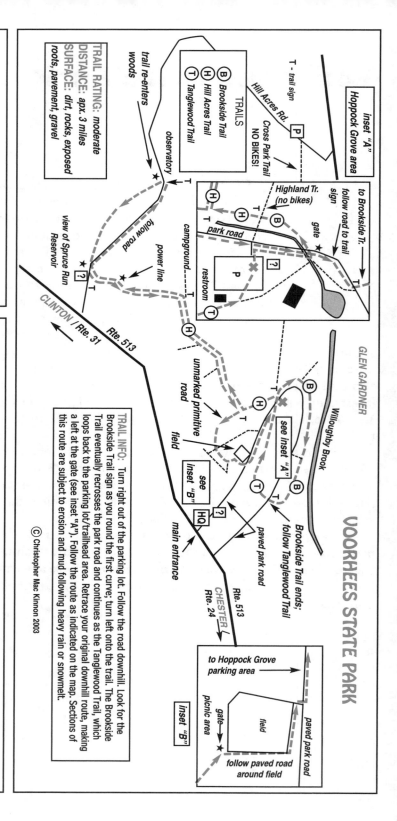

VOORHEES STATE PARK

inset "A"
Hoppock Grove area

GLEN GARDNER

Voorhees State Park
Route 513
Glen Gardner
Hunterdon County
908-638-6969

TRAIL RATING: moderate
DISTANCE: apx 3 miles
SURFACE: dirt, rocks, exposed roots, pavement, gravel

TRAILS
- (B) Brookside Trail
- (H) Hill Acres Trail
- (T) Tanglewood Trail

T - trail sign

trail re-enters woods

observatory

Cross Park Trail
NO BIKES!

Hill Acres Rd.

to Brookside Tr.
follow road to trail

T sign

Highland Tr.
(no bikes)

gate

park road

campground

power line

restroom

follow road

view of Spruce Run
Reservoir

unmarked primitive road

field

CLINTON / Rte. 31

Rte. 513

Willoughby Brook

Brookside Trail ends;
follow Tanglewood Trail

see inset "A"

see inset "B"

paved park road

HQ

main entrance

CHESTER
Rte. 24

Rte. 513

© Christopher Mac Kinnon 2003

TRAIL INFO: Turn right out of the parking lot. Follow the road downhill. Look for the Brookside Trail sign as you round the first curve; turn left onto the trail. The Brookside Trail eventually recrosses the park road and continues as the Tanglewood Trail, which loops back to the parking lot/trailhead area. Retrace your original downhill route, making a left at the gate (see inset "A"). Follow the route as indicated on the map. Sections of this route are subject to erosion and mud following heavy rain or snowmelt.

Directions: From Route 78, take Route 31 (Exit 17) north almost 2 miles to Route 513 north. Follow Route 513 through the town of High Bridge to the park, which is located about 2 miles north of town. The Hoppock Grove parking area is located approximately half a mile in from the main entrance to the park.

inset "B"
to Hoppock Grove
parking area

gate

field

picnic area

paved park road

follow paved road
around field

Notes:

Sign at Washington Crossing State Park

Washington Crossing State Park

Washington Crossing State Park, a well known historical destination, only recently has opened some of its trails
to mountain bikes.

The park-designated bike route begins at the Phillips
Farm area off Route 579 (Bear Tavern Road). There are
several farm buildings adjacent to the parking lot. To find
the trail, go behind the buildings and look for a brown
trail sign. A green-and-white trail sign should be visible in
the distance where the field ends and the woods begin.
Follow the grassy path around the perimeter of the field
to this point. With the addition of new markers, it has become somewhat
easier to navigate through this area.

At the point where the grassy path intersects a gravel road, go around
the gate and turn left onto Brickyard Road. (Refer to map inset "B.") Follow
Brickyard Road until you reach the main paved road through the park. (Refer to inset "A.") If time permits, stop at the park visitor center, where you'll
find exhibits illustrating the historical significance of George Washington's
crossing of the Delaware River with the Continental Army on Christmas in
1776, a turning point in the Revolutionary War.

When you're done, take the park road back to Brick Yard Road and follow it to the interpretive center, which houses a collection of exhibits relat-
ing to many varieties of wildlife in the park and around New Jersey.

From the interpretive center, backtrack again to Brickyard Road. At this
point, the singletrack portion of the ride begins and ends. (Refer to the map
for the route through this segment.) When you find yourself back where
the singletrack section started, turn left onto Brickyard Road, then left again
past the gate, following the gravel road back to the Phillips Farm area.

This ride is rated as moderate because of the singletrack section. Both
the road and grassy paths are suited for the casual rider.

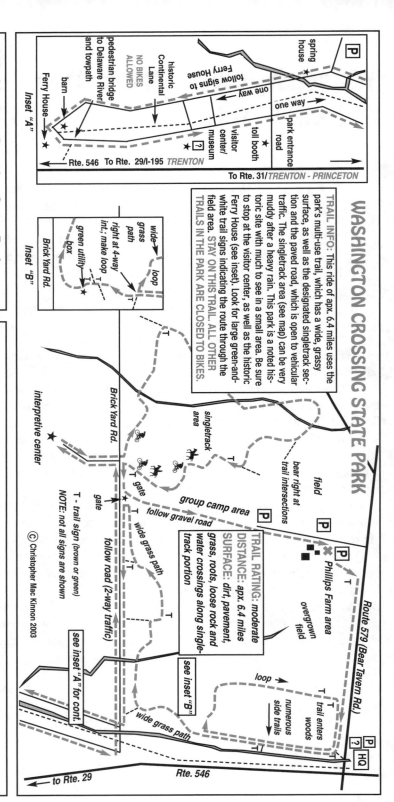

WASHINGTON CROSSING STATE PARK

TRAIL INFO: This ride of apx. 6.4 miles uses the park's multi-use trail, which has a wide, grassy surface, as well as the designated singletrack section and the paved road, which is open to vehicular traffic. The singletrack area (see map) can be very muddy after a heavy rain. This park is a noted historic site with much to see in a small area. Be sure to stop at the visitor center, as well as the historic Ferry House (see inset). Look for large green-and-white trail signs indicating the route through the field area. **STAY ON THIS TRAIL. ALL OTHER TRAILS IN THE PARK ARE CLOSED TO BIKES.**

TRAIL RATING: moderate
DISTANCE: apx. 6.4 miles
SURFACE: dirt, pavement, grass, roots, loose rock and water crossings along single-track portion

Inset "A"

Inset "B"

Brick Yard Rd.

wide grass path

green utility box

right at 4-way int; make loop

loop

spring house

follow signs to Ferry House

one way

park entrance road

one way

historic Continental Lane
NO BIKES ALLOWED

Ferry House

barn

pedestrian bridge to Delaware River and towpath

visitor center/ museum

toll booth

Rte. 546 To Rte. 29/I-195 *TRENTON*

To Rte. 31/ *TRENTON - PRINCETON*

singletrack area

bear right at trail intersections

field

Brick Yard Rd.

interpretive center

© Christopher Mac Kinnon 2003

gate

gate

group camp area

follow gravel road

T - trail sign (brown or green)
NOTE: not all signs are shown

wide grass path

follow road (2-way traffic)

see inset "A" for cont.

see inset "B"

wide grass path

Phillips Farm area

overgrown field

Route 579 (Bear Tavern Rd.)

loop

numerous side trails

woods

trail enters

to Rte. 29

Rte. 546

HQ

Washington Crossing State Park
off Route 546 (Washington Crossing-Pennington Road)
Titusville
Mercer County
609-737-0623

Directions: From I-95, take Exit 2 and go north on Route 579 (Bear Tavern Road). Bear right and then left at Jacob's Creek Road to stay on Route 579. The entrance to the Phillips Farm area of the park is on the left past the traffic light at Route 546 (Washington Crossing-Pennington Road), about 2.7 miles north of I-95.

Washington Valley Park

Washington Valley is not the same kind of destination as High Point State Park or Round Valley Reservoir, with their obvious attractions and family-oriented recreational facilities. Instead, you could think of it as those woods across the street where you used to play ... only much bigger!

Washington Valley Park, also known as White Rocks or Chimney Rock and shown on some county maps as the Watchung Reservation, has much to offer the off-road enthusiast. The park includes about 2,000 acres with an extensive network of trails to explore, many of which are in the form of rocky, steep, twisting, unforgiving singletrack. This secluded gem is a prime area for mountain biking in New Jersey and, hopefully, development and restrictions will be kept to a minimum in the future.

Except for the posted Somerset County parks signs loosely defining the perimeter of the park, there is little at Washington Valley to indicate county ownership. As you explore the network of singletrack trails, dirt paths, and gravel roads that combine to make up the route, you might get the feeling that this area is an extension of the many backyards that are adjacent to the trail. Diplomacy and trail etiquette are highly recommended here! Locals seem to be very protective of the area. Be a positive representative for your sport; if you are not sure about area boundaries, ask or select an alternate route.

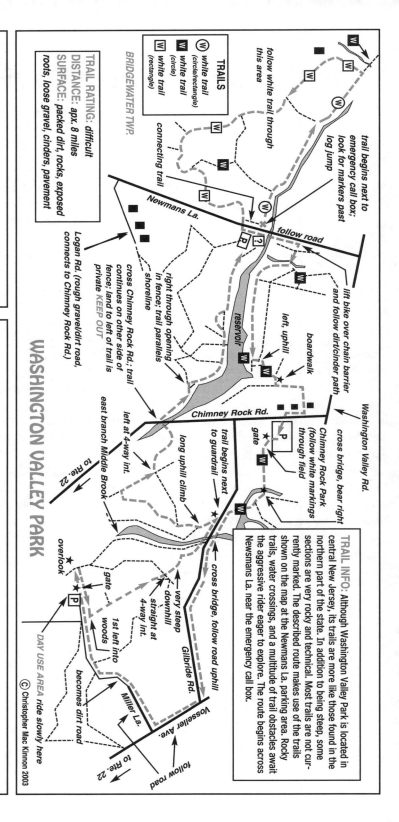

Washington Valley Park
off Chimney Rock Road
Martinsville
Somerset County
908-722-1200

Directions: From Route 22, follow Chimney Rock Road 2 miles to Washington Valley Road. Turn left on Washington Valley, then left again onto Newmans Lane. Cross the bridge and turn left into the parking area.

WASHINGTON VALLEY PARK

BRIDGEWATER TWP.

TRAILS
- (W) white trail (circle/rectangle)
- [W] white trail (circle)
- [W] white trail (rectangle)

TRAIL RATING: difficult
DISTANCE: apx. 8 miles
SURFACE: packed dirt, rocks, exposed roots, loose gravel, cinders, pavement

trail begins next to emergency call box; look for markers past log jump

follow white trail through this area

connecting trail

Newmans La.

follow road

lift bike over chain barrier and follow dirt/cinder path

Logan Rd. (rough gravel/dirt road, connects to Chimney Rock Rd.)

right through opening in fence; trail parallels shoreline

cross Chimney Rock Rd.: trail continues on other side of fence; land to left of trail is private KEEP OUT

reservoir

left, uphill

boardwalk

Washington Valley Rd.

cross bridge, bear right

Chimney Rock Park (follow white markings through field

gate

Chimney Rock Rd.

left at 4-way int.

long uphill climb

east branch Middle Brook

to Rte. 22

trail begins next to guardrail

cross bridge, follow road uphill

Gilbride Rd.

very steep downhill

straight at 4-way int.

1st left into woods

overlook

gate

DAY USE AREA ride slowly here

becomes dirt road

Vosseller Ave.

Miller La.

to Rte. 22

follow road

TRAIL INFO: Although Washington Valley Park is located in central New Jersey, its trails are more like those found in the northern part of the state. In addition to being steep, some sections are very rocky and technical. Most trails are not currently marked. The described route makes use of the trails shown on the map at the Newmans La. parking area. Rocky trails, water crossings, and a multitude of trail obstacles await the aggressive rider eager to explore. The route begins across Newmans La. near the emergency call box.

© Christopher Mac Kinnon 2003

Wawayanda State Park

Before it became a state park in 1963, Wawayanda's vast natural resources provided a source of income for the iron and logging industries. Present-day Wawayanda is a prime location for outdoor recreation in northern New Jersey.

Wawayanda, located near the New York border, has a reputation for being more "biker friendly" than many other locations. Forest roads built for use by loggers are now part of this 13,000-acre park's extensive system of trails, most of them open to mountain bikers. The variety of terrain encountered along these trails is diverse, including lush woods, rock outcroppings, and wetlands.

The focal point for many visitors to the park is 250-acre Wawayanda Lake with its scenic backdrop of forested hills. The lake is open for swimming in the summer, and there are changing facilities nearby. Canoes and boats with electric motors are also allowed, and fishing is popular. A nearby charcoal blast furnace serves as a reminder of a once-thriving iron industry (see map for location). If you simply want to cycle, park at the first lot next to the park headquarters. By doing so, you can avoid paying a toll for lake parking.

Before beginning your ride, stop in at the park headquarters for information on trail conditions, revisions, etc.

Wawayanda State Park
Warwick Turnpike (Route 511)
Wawayanda
Sussex County
973-853-4462

TRAIL RATING: *difficult*
DISTANCE: *apx. 12 miles*
SURFACE: *packed dirt, rock, roots, mud, pavement*

THIS SECTION OF THE IRON MTN. TRAIL IS ALSO THE APPALACHIAN TRAIL

turn right at Iron Mtn. Tr. sign onto Crossover Rd.

turn right at 3-way int.; trail follows dirt road

NY

NJ

bridge ★

Iron Mtn. Rd.

Old Wawayanda Rd.

P
HQ
?

TRAILS
Ⓨ Laurel Pond - Yellow
Ⓑ Hoeferlin - Blue
Ⓨ Double Pond - Yellow
Ⓡ Red Dot - Red
Ⓘ Iron Mtn. - Red/White Rectangle

Wawayanda Rd.

inset

trail is primitive road here

Waywayanda Rd.

Ⓘ

Iron Mtn. Tr.
Wawayanda Rd.

P

trail starts at rear of parking area by picnic table; narrow single-track; may be overgrown

P

trail starts opposite park HQ bldg.

Ⓑ

© Christopher Mac Kinnon 2003

Ⓘ

Ⓘ

see inset of this area

beach area

gravel path

furnace

lake

gate ★

Ⓨ

Warwick Tpk.

Wawayanda Lake

Ⓨ

to Rtes. 513/23

WAWAYANDA
STATE PARK

sign ★

Ⓨ

sign ★

Ⓑ

Ⓨ

Ⓨ

Ⓡ

Ⓡ

Ⓡ

sign ★

Ⓨ

Cherry Ridge Rd.

Cherry Ridge Rd.

Ⓡ

left at "T"

← singletrack

Banker Tr.

Clinton Rd.

to Rte. 23 NEWFOUNDLAND

★ sign

sign ★

Cherry Ridge Rd.

Directions: From Route 23 in Newfoundland, go north on Union Valley Road about 9 miles through West Milford to Warwick Turnpike (Route 511). Turn left onto Warwick Turnpike and follow signs to Wawayanda State Park. Park next to the headquarters building.

TRAIL INFO: This ride of about 12 miles through Wawayanda State Park follows some of the more popular trails as well as the less frequently used Red Dot Trail. Most of this route follows wide doubletrack trails or uses some of the primitive roads within the park. CAUTION: BE ALERT FOR POSSIBLE VEHICULAR TRAFFIC ALONG CHERRY RIDGE, OLD WAWAYANDA, AND IRON MOUNTAIN RDS. Short stretches of challenging singletrack can be found along the Red Dot Trail and the Iron Mountain Trail near the beach parking lot. The blast furnace (see map) is a remnant from a once-thriving iron industry. BEFORE BEGINNING THIS RIDE STOP BY THE PARK HEADQUARTERS FOR A GENERAL PARK MAP AND A TRAIL LIST INDICATING WHICH TRAILS ARE CLOSED TO BIKES. Bike parking is allowed in the lot next to the park office.

Wells Mills County Park

This 900-acre tract in the Pinelands of Ocean County is home to a variety of environments typical of this region. Streams, bogs, swamps, and uplands combine to make the park itself a living museum.

Before beginning your ride, stop by the park office/nature center. The observation deck located in this building provides a panoramic view of the surrounding Pine Barrens. Exhibits in this architecturally appealing structure offer a comprehensive look into Pinelands culture, traditions, and ecosystems.

Wells Mills is the largest park in the Ocean County Park System, and it has a total of about 16 miles of trails, but the trails indicated on the route map are the only ones where bikes were permitted at the time of publication. Inquire at the office about whether any additional trails have been designated for or opened to mountain biking.

Ridge and Cooks Mills Roads are easily recognizable, being considerably wider than the numerous intersecting trails. Look for both green blazes and a small metallic sign with a bike symbol and directional arrow.

Wells Mills is a multi-use park. In addition to the network of trails, Wells Mills Lake is open for fishing and boating (electric motors only). The park also rents canoes on a seasonal basis, and the Pine Barrens Jamboree, a celebration of local culture, is held here each October.

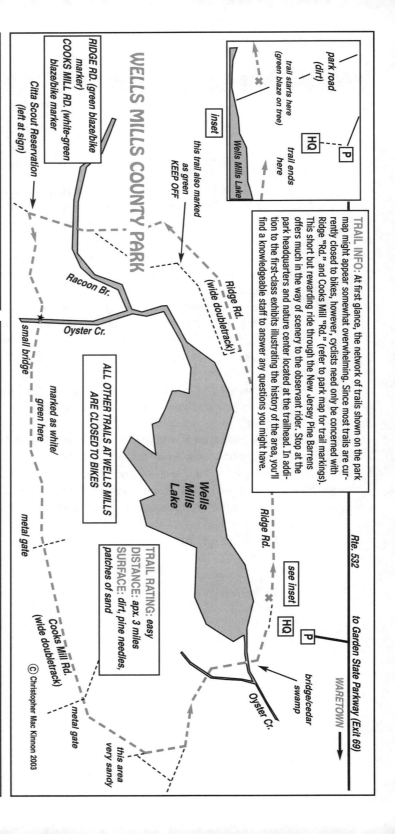

WELLS MILLS COUNTY PARK

inset

park road (dirt)

trail starts here (green blaze on tree)

trail ends here

P

HQ

Wells Mills Lake

RIDGE RD. (green blaze/bike marker)
COOKS MILL RD. (white-green blaze/bike marker)

Citta Scout Reservation (left at sign)

this trail also marked as green KEEP OFF

Racoon Br.

Oyster Cr.

Ridge Rd. (wide doubletrack)

ALL OTHER TRAILS AT WELLS MILLS ARE CLOSED TO BIKES

small bridge

marked as white/green here

metal gate

Wells Mills Lake

© Christopher Mac Kinnon 2003

TRAIL RATING: easy
DISTANCE: apx. 3 miles
SURFACE: dirt, pine needles, patches of sand

metal gate

Cooks Mill Rd. (wide doubletrack)

this area very sandy

Oyster Cr.

bridge/cedar swamp

see inset

P

HQ

Ridge Rd.

Rte. 532   **to Garden State Parkway (Exit 69)**

WARETOWN ➡

TRAIL INFO: At first glance, the network of trails shown on the park map might appear somewhat overwhelming. Since most trails are currently closed to bikes, however, cyclists need only be concerned with Ridge "Rd." and Cooks Mill "Rd." (refer to park map for trail markings). This short but rewarding ride through the New Jersey Pine Barrens offers much in the way of scenery to the observant rider. Stop at the park headquarters and nature center located at the trailhead. In addition to the first-class exhibits illustrating the history of the area, you'll find a knowledgeable staff to answer any questions you might have.

Wells Mills County Park
Route 532 (Wells Mills Road)
Waretown
Ocean County
609-971-3085

Directions: From the north, take the Garden State Parkway south to Exit 67. Turn right onto Route 554 (West Bay Avenue) and continue about 5 miles to Route 532. Turn right onto Route 532 and continue 3 miles to the park entrance on the right. From the south, take the parkway north to Exit 69. Turn left onto Route 532 (west) and continue about 2 miles to the park entrance on the left.

West Essex Rail Trail

Considering its urban location, this trail is a jewel in the rough, offering what might be the longest legal off-road cycling opportunity in the Essex-Hudson County area.

You won't find technical singletrack or monster hill climbs here, but the trail does offer some relief from traffic and noise pollution.

This is an out-and-back route on one of New Jersey's least known and only moderately used rail trails. Although located in the heavily urbanized part of the state, the trail passes through sections of woodland, providing a short escape from the surrounding congestion.

Unfortunately, the most scenic section of the trail is currently in disrepair. Refer to the Pompton Avenue/Community Park area inset on the trail map for the location of the trestle that once carried heavy loads over the Peckman River. Because the trestle is currently in poor condition, using it to cross the river is highly discouraged. Refer to the map inset to bypass this area.

A picturesque view of the river is available at the point where you leave Community Park crossing a small bridge connecting to Little Falls Road.

West Essex Rail Trail
Verona to Little Falls
Essex and Passaic Counties
973-268-3500

Directions: From Pompton Avenue/Route 23, turn onto Little Falls Road. Go about half a mile to Community Park. Turn right into the park.

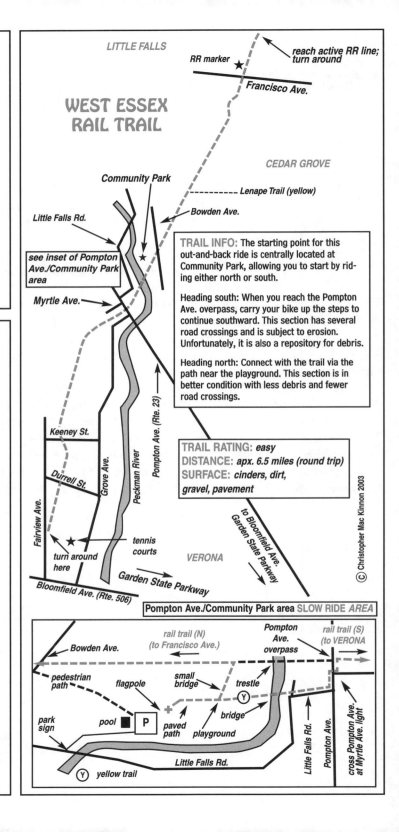

LITTLE FALLS

RR marker ★ — reach active RR line; turn around

Francisco Ave.

WEST ESSEX RAIL TRAIL

CEDAR GROVE

Community Park

- - - - - - - Lenape Trail (yellow)

Bowden Ave.

Little Falls Rd.

★

see inset of Pompton Ave./Community Park area

Myrtle Ave.

TRAIL INFO: The starting point for this out-and-back ride is centrally located at Community Park, allowing you to start by riding either north or south.

Heading south: When you reach the Pompton Ave. overpass, carry your bike up the steps to continue southward. This section has several road crossings and is subject to erosion. Unfortunately, it is also a repository for debris.

Heading north: Connect with the trail via the path near the playground. This section is in better condition with less debris and fewer road crossings.

Keeney St.

Durrell St.

Fairview Ave.

Grove Ave.

Peckman River

Pompton Ave. (Rte. 23)

TRAIL RATING: *easy*
DISTANCE: *apx. 6.5 miles (round trip)*
SURFACE: *cinders, dirt, gravel, pavement*

© Christopher Mac Kinnon 2003

to Bloomfield Ave. Garden State Parkway

★ tennis courts

turn around here

VERONA

Garden State Parkway

Bloomfield Ave. (Rte. 506)

Pompton Ave./Community Park area SLOW RIDE *AREA*

rail trail (N) (to Francisco Ave.)

Pompton Ave. overpass

rail trail (S) (to VERONA

Bowden Ave.

pedestrian path

flagpole

small bridge

trestle

Ⓨ

cross Pompton Ave. at Myrtle Ave. light

park sign

pool ■ P

paved path

bridge

playground

Little Falls Rd.

Pompton Ave.

Little Falls Rd.

Ⓨ yellow trail

Get involved

Biking advocacy groups have played a major role in the success our sport enjoys today. The design and maintenance of trails and education of trail users are crucial factors contributing to the growth and enjoyment of the off-road cycling experience. These organizations depend on the contributions of many dedicated volunteers to accomplish their goals.

Two national cycling-advocacy organizations have led the way:

International Mountain Bicycling Association (IMBA)
www.imba.com

National Off-Road Bicycling Association (NORBA)
www.usacycling.org/mtb/

This group is active on the state level:

Jersey Off-Road Bicycling Association (JORBA)
www.jorba.info

A number of regional or local groups share the objectives of these larger organizations. Bikeable trails at Allaire, Mercer County Park, and Atlantic County Park are the direct result of the work of their volunteers.

Allaire Trail Users Group (ATUG)
home.att.net/~atug/

A coalition of bikers, hikers, hunters, and equestrians who have come together to work for a common cause. The organization was formed in response to threatened trail closures at Allaire State Park in 1998.

ATUG is responsible for maintaining existing trails at the park and has been instrumental in the design and construction of new trails. The organization welcomes new members to help ensure that this area remains open in the future.

Save Mercer and Ride the Trails (SMART)
www.angelfire.com/nj2/smart17/

A mountain-bike advocacy group dedicated to maintaining and improving the off-road trails in Mercer County Park in West Windsor. One of SMART's most significant accomplishments has been to map and mark the many off-road trails in the park, a project that took place during the summer of 2002.

The organization schedules trail maintenance days on the third Saturday of each month. SMART, which was founded in 1999, is affiliated with both IMBA and JORBA. Members pay a small fee to belong, and the group also has the support of a few local businesses. The Mercer County Bicycle Patrol is another volunteer group that operates in Mercer County Park. Members are CPR certified and belong to the National Mountain Bike Patrol.

Atlantic County Trail Volunteers (ACTV)
www.geocities.com/actv03/

A volunteer organization that has brought together recreational mountain bikers and hikers to address trail issues in Atlantic County. The organization designs, builds, and maintains environmentally conscious and safe singletrack trail systems.

Contact us

Let us know what you think of these routes. Tell us if trail conditions have changed, or if you have new information to add. We'll post any updates we receive on the Freewheeling Press Web site.

Also, tell us about your own favorite bicycling routes. (They don't have to be in New Jersey.) Rides suggested by readers may be included on our Web site or in future editions of this or other bicycle tour books.

Write to us at:

Freewheeling Press
P.O. Box 540
Lahaska PA 18931

You can also reach us via e-mail:

info@freewheelingpress.com

You'll find useful information about bicycling in New Jersey and news about what's happening here at Freewheeling Press on our Web site:

www.freewheelingpress.com

Buy a book

Use this form to order books from Freewheeling Press, or look for more information about ordering online at www.freewheelingpress.com.

Name:

Address:

Telephone:

No.	Title	Price	Total
	Back Roads Bicycling in Bucks County, Pa. *Features more than 40 rides on bike paths and scenic roads, with detailed maps and descriptions in a bike-friendly format.*	$14.95	
	Mountain Biking in New Jersey *More than 40 off-road rides in the Garden State, each accompanied by descriptive text and a detailed map with everything you need to know to enjoy each ride.*	$14.95	
	Walking Bucks County, Pa. *A guide to walks on country roads, paved paths, and woodland trails in this scenic area, with maps.*	$12.95	
	Freewheeling Press Bike Journal *Personal bike touring journal opens flat for easy writing, with space to record directions, distance, difficulty, and other details of your rides.*	$12.95	
	The Back Roads Bike Book *Maps and directions for a dozen short scenic rides in and around Lambertville, N.J., and New Hope, Pa., with info on things to see and do, places to stay.*	$12.95	

Send to: **Freewheeling Press PO Box 540 Lahaska PA 18931**	Shipping ($2 per book)	
	Subtotal	
	Pa. residents add 6% tax	
	Grand total	
	Make check payable to Freewheeling Press	